United States
Department of
Agriculture

Forest Service

**Northern
Research Station**

Resource Bulletin
NRS-44

Kansas's Forests, 2005: Statistics, Methods and Quality Assurance

Patrick D. Miles, W. Keith Moser,
Charles J. Barnett

Abstract

The first full annual inventory of Kansas's forests was completed in 2005 after 8,868 plots were selected and 468 forested plots were visited and measured. This report includes detailed information on forest inventory methods and data quality estimates. Important resource statistics are included in the tables. A detailed analysis of the Kansas inventory is presented in Resource Bulletin NRS-26 (www.nrs.fs.fed.us/pubs/rb/rb_nrs26.pdf).

The Authors

Patrick D. Miles and Warren K. Moser are research foresters with the Forest Inventory and Analysis program, Northern Research Station, St. Paul, Minnesota.

Charles J. Barnett is a forester with the Forest Inventory and Analysis program, Northern Research Station, Newtown Square, PA.

CONTENTS

FOREST INVENTORY METHODS
Strategic Model

The Forest Inventory and Analysis (FIA) program of the Northern Research Station (NRS) is part of the national enhanced FIA program that focuses on six strategic objectives (McRoberts 2005):

- A standard set of variables with nationally consistent meanings and measurements.
- Field inventories of all forested lands.
- Nationally consistent estimation.
- Adherence to national precision standards.
- Consistent reporting and data distribution.
- Credibility with users and stakeholders.

To ensure that these objectives are achieved, 10 strategic approaches have been prescribed:

- A national set of prescribed core variables with a national field manual that describes measurement procedures and protocols for each variable.
- A national plot configuration.
- A nationally consistent sampling design.
- Estimation using standardized formulae for sample-based estimators.
- A national database of FIA data with core standards and user-friendly public access.
- A national information management system.
- A nationally consistent set of tables with estimates of prescribed core variables.
- Publication of statewide tables with estimates of prescribed core variables at 5-year intervals.
- Documentation of the technical aspects of the FIA program including procedures, protocols, and techniques.
- Peer review and publication of the technical documentation for general access.

The result of this approach is an inventory program with new features and a nationally consistent plot configuration, a nationally consistent sampling design for all lands, annual measurement of a proportion of plots in each state, nationally consistent estimation techniques and algorithms, and integration of the ground-sampling components of the FIA inventory and detection monitoring by the USDA Forest Service's Forest Health Monitoring (FHM) program.

Plot Configuration

The national FIA plot design (Fig. 1) consists of four circular 24-ft-radius subplots (1/24th acre) configured as a central subplot and three peripheral subplots. Centers of the peripheral subplots are 120 ft from the central subplot and at azimuths of 360°, 120°, and 240° from the center of the central subplot. Trees with a diameter at breast height (d.b.h.) of 5 inches or greater are measured on these subplots. Each subplot contains a circular 6.8-ft-radius microplot (1/300th acre) with the center located 12 ft east of the subplot center on which each tree at least 1 inch but less than 5 inches d.b.h. is measured. Forest conditions that occur on any of the four subplots are identified and recorded; if the area of the condition is 1 acre or greater, the condition is mapped on the subplot. Factors that differentiate forest conditions include forest type, stand-size class, stand origin, land use, ownership, and density. Macroplots are not used by NRS-FIA. They have a radius of 58.9 ft and are used for sampling intensification or for sampling relatively rare events. The ¼- acre macroplot currently is used by the Rocky Mountain and Pacific Northwest Stations' FIA programs to sample large trees.

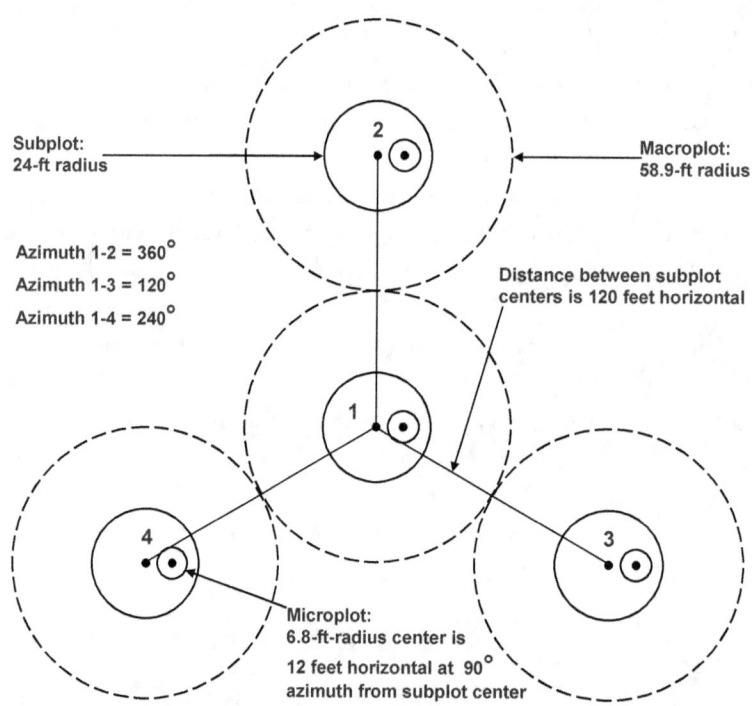

Subplot:
24-ft radius

Macroplot:
58.9-ft radius

Azimuth 1-2 = 360°

Azimuth 1-3 = 120°

Azimuth 1-4 = 240°

Distance between subplot centers is 120 feet horizontal

Microplot:
6.8-ft-radius center is
12 feet horizontal at 90°
azimuth from subplot center

Figure 1.—National FIA plot design (adapted from Bechtold and Patterson 2005).

Sample Design

On the basis of historical sampling errors, a sampling intensity of about one plot per 6,000 acres is necessary to satisfy national FIA precision guidelines. Therefore, FIA divided the area of the United States into nonoverlapping, 5,937-acre hexagons and, for Kansas, established a plot at a random location in the hexagon. This array of field plots is designated the Federal base sample and is considered an equal probability sample; measurement of the Federal base sample is funded by the Federal Government.

The Federal base sample is divided into five interpenetrating, nonoverlapping panels or subsamples, each of which provides complete, systematic coverage of a state. Each year, plots in a single panel are measured; panels are selected on a 5-year, rotating basis (McRoberts 1999). For estimation purposes, the measurement of each panel of plots is considered an independent, equal probability sample of all lands in a state.

Three-Phase Inventory

FIA conducts inventories in three phases. Remotely sensed data are used in Phase 1 to obtain initial plot land-cover observations to determine whether a field visit is required. Phase 1 data also are used to classify total area in the population of interest, for latter use in the post-stratification process, to increase the precision of estimates. In Phase 2, field crews visit the physical locations of permanent field plots to measure traditional inventory variables such as tree species, diameter, and height. In Phase 3, field crews visit a subset of Phase 2 plots to obtain measurements for an additional suite of variables associated with forest and ecosystem health. The three phases of the enhanced FIA program as implemented in this inventory are discussed in detail in the sections that follow.

Phase 1

Aerial photographs, digital orthoquads (DOQs: digitally scanned aerial photograph), and satellite imagery are used for initial plot measurement via remotely sensed data and stratification. Phase 1 plot measurement consists of observations of conditions at the plot locations using aerial photographs or DOQs. Analysts determine a digitized geographic location for each field plot and a human interpreter assigns to the plot a land cover/use with primary focus on identifying forest land.[1] All plot locations that could contain forest land are selected for further measurement via field-crew visits in Phase 2.

The combination of natural variability among plots and budgetary constraints prohibits measurement of a sufficient number of plots to satisfy national precision standards for most inventory variables unless the estimation process is enhanced using ancillary data. Thus, the land area is stratified using remotely sensed and other map-based data.

A stratification scheme based on satellite imagery as proposed by Hansen and Wendt (2000) is applied to the National Land Cover Data (NLCD) as suggested by McRoberts et al. (2002). The NLCD is a digital land-cover map of the conterminous United States in which 30- by 30-m pixels are assigned to 21 land-cover classes. This classification was produced by the U.S. Geological Survey and was based on nominal 1992 Landsat 5 Thematic Mapper (TM) satellite imagery and ancillary data (Vogelmann et al. 2001). Four strata are created using a three-step process: 1) aggregate NLCD classes with trees into a forest stratum with the remaining classes into a nonforest stratum; 2) reclassify isolated groups of three or fewer pixels into their surrounding forest or nonforest class to comply with the FIA criterion that forest land must be at least 1 acre; and 3) create two additional classes (forest edge and nonforest edge) that includes all pixels within two pixels of the forest/nonforest boundary.

---

[1]Lands satisfying FIA's definition of forest land include commercial timberland, some pastured land with trees, forest plantations, unproductive forested land, and reserved, noncommercial forested land. Forest land requires minimum stocking levels, a 1-acre minimum area, and a minimum bole-to-bole width of 120 ft. with continuous canopy. Forest land excludes wooded strips and windbreaks less than 120 ft. wide and idle farmland or other previously nonforest land that currently is below minimum stocking levels.

In addition to classifying every pixel into one of the four strata, every pixel is assigned to an ownership stratum based on the Protected Areas Database (PAD) described by DellaSala et al. (2001). In Kansas, PAD was used to classify pixels into two ownership classes. Based on the pixel counts for Kansas there are 52,349,981 acres of private land and 307,301 acres of public land.

Stratified estimation requires that two tasks be accomplished. First, each plot must be assigned to a single stratum. Next, the proportion of each detailed stratum must be calculated (TM land-cover classification and ownership group delineation). The first task is accomplished by assigning each plot to the stratum assigned for the pixel containing the center of the center subplot. The second task is accomplished by calculating the proportion of pixels in each stratum. The population estimate for a variable is calculated as the sum across all strata of the product of each stratum's observed proportion (from Phase 1) and the variable's estimated mean per unit area for the stratum (from Phase 2). The stratum assignments used in Kansas are discussed in the estimation section of this report.

Phase 2

In Phase 2, field crews record a variety of data for plot locations determined in Phase 1 to include accessible forest land. Before visiting plot locations, field crews consult county land records to determine the ownership of plots and then seek permission from private landowners to measure plots on their lands. At the plot, field crews determine the location of the geographic center of the center subplot using (GPS) receivers. They record condition-level observations that include land cover, forest type, stand origin, stand age, stand-size class, site-productivity class, history of forest disturbance, and land use for every condition (major land use or forest stand at least 1 acre in size) that occurs on the plot. They also record information on condition boundaries on plots with multiple conditions. For each tree, field crews record a variety of observations and measurements, including condition, species, live/dead status, lean, diameter, height, crown ratio (percentage of tree height represented by crown), crown class (dominant, codominant, suppressed), damage, and decay status. Office staff use statistical models based on field-crew measurements to calculate values for additional variables, including individual-tree volume, per-unit-area estimates of number of trees, volume, and biomass by plot, condition, species group, and live/dead status. Additional information on data collection procedures used in Phase 2 is available at http://www.nrs.fs.fed.us/fia/data-collection/.

Phase 3

The third phase of the enhanced FIA program focuses on forest health. Phase 3 is administered by the FIA program with consultation from other Forest Service programs, other Federal agencies, state natural resource agencies, universities, and the FHM program. The FHM program consists of four interrelated and complementary activities: detection, evaluation, intensive site-ecosystem monitoring, and research on monitoring techniques. Detection monitoring consists of systematic aerial and ground surveys designed to collect baseline information on the current condition of forest ecosystems and to detect changes from those baselines over time. Evaluation studies examine the extent, severity, and probable causes of changes in forest health identified through the detection monitoring surveys. Intensive site-ecosystem monitoring examines regionally specific ecological processes at a network of sites in representative forested ecosystems. Research on monitoring techniques focuses on developing and refining indicator measurements to improve the efficiency and reliability of data collection and analysis at all levels of the program.

The ground-survey portion of the detection-monitoring program was integrated into the FIA program as Phase 3 in 1999. The Phase 3 sample consists of a 1:16 subset of the Phase 2 plots with one Phase 3 plot for about every 95,000 acres. Phase 3 measurements are obtained by field crews during the growing season and include an extended suite of ecological data: lichen diversity and abundance, soil quality (erosion, compaction, and chemistry), vegetation diversity and structure, and down woody material. The incidence and severity of ozone injury for selected bioindicator species also are monitored as part of an associated sampling scheme. All Phase 2 measurements are collected on each Phase 3 plot at the same time as the Phase 3 measurements. Additional information on data-collection procedures used in Phase 3 is available at http://www.nrs.fs.fed.us/fia/topics/.

Phase 3 variables are selected to address specific criteria outlined by the Montreal Process Working Group for the conservation and sustainable management of temperate and boreal forests (Montreal Process 1995) and are based on the concept of indicator variables. Observations of an indicator variable represent an index of ecosystem functions that can be monitored over time to assess trends. Indicator variables are used in conjunction with each other, Phase 2 data, data from FHM evaluation monitoring studies, and ancillary data to address ecological issues such as vegetation diversity, fuel loading, regional air-quality gradients, and carbon storage. The Phase 2 and 3 data of the enhanced FIA program are a primary source of reporting data for the Montreal Process Criteria.

Estimation

Most of the estimates and analysis of forest resources in this report, including the estimates in Tables 1-20, 31-32, 54-59a, and 65 are based on data collected on the 8,868 Phase 2 plots across Kansas (Fig. 2). The analysis of forest health issues that relate to down woody materials, soils, ozone damage, and crown condition are based on data collected on the 519 Phase 3 plots (Fig. 3).

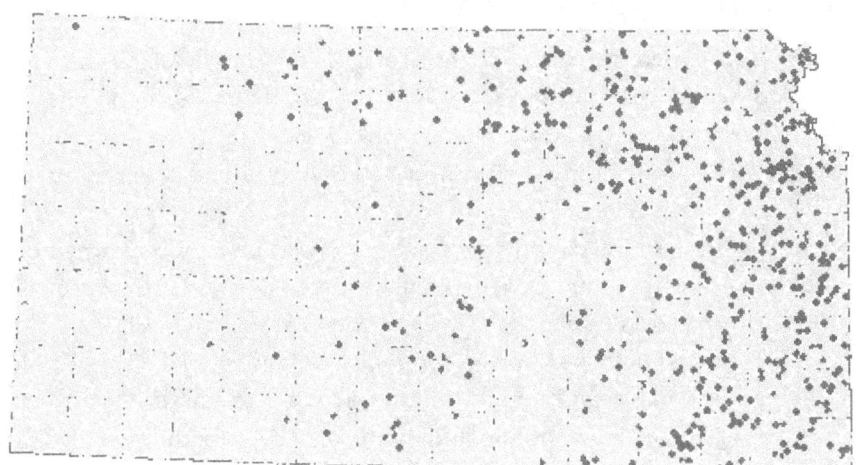

Figure 2.—Approximate location of forest-land (green dots) and nonforest land (yellow dots) Phase 2 plots, Kansas, 2005.

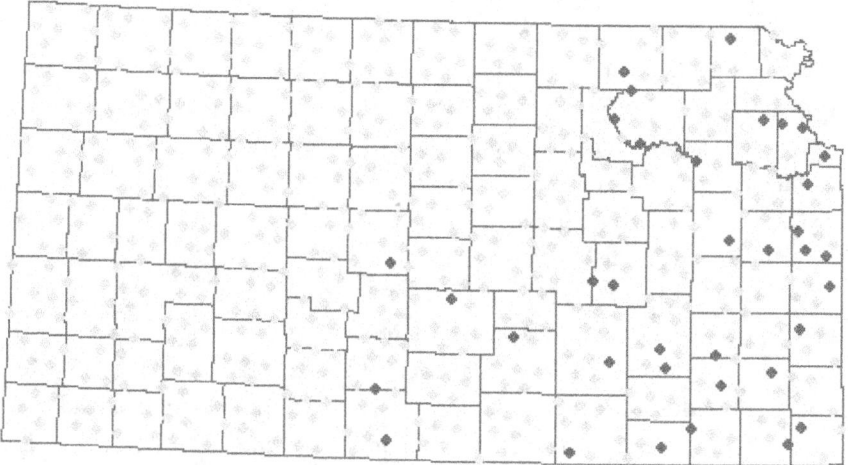

Figure 3.—Approximate location of forest-land (green dots) and nonforest land (yellow dots) Phase 3 plots, Kansas, 2005.

About 20 percent of the Phase 2 observations were acquired each year from October 1, 2000 to September 30, 2005. These observations, collectively called the 2005 inventory, are within 14 estimation strata (Table A) defined by combinations of the four Phase 1 classes (nonforest, nonforest edge, forest edge, and forest), a land-ownership classification created from the PAD and forest-survey units. Procedures described in Bechtold and Patterson (2005) for stratified estimation with observed stratum areas were used in conjunction with the strata in Table A to produce all estimates. The total area and number of plots within each stratum is shown in Table A.

Integration with Previous Inventories

In 2005, FIA completed measurement of the fifth panel of inventory plots in Kansas. The 2005 panel along with those surveyed in 2001, 2002, 2003, and 2004 comprise the dataset for the fourth inventory of Kansas's forests (Moser et al. 2008). Previous inventories of Kansas's forest resources were completed in 1965, 1980, and 1994 (Chase and Strickler 1968, Spencer et al. 1984, and Leatherberry et al. 1999).

Data from new inventories often are compared with data from earlier inventories to determine trends in forest resources. However, for the comparisons to be valid, the procedures used in the two inventories must be similar. As a result of our ongoing efforts to improve the efficiency and reliability of the inventory, there have been several changes in procedures and definitions since the 1994 Kansas inventory. These changes will have little impact on statewide estimates of forest area, timber volume, and tree biomass but they may significantly affect condition-classification variables such as forest type and stand-size class.

For consistency, a new, national plot design was implemented by all five regional FIA units in 1999 in which fixed-radius subplots are used exclusively. Prior to the new plot design, (during the 1980 and 1994 inventories) fixed and variable-radius subplots were used. Both designs have strong points but they often produce different classifications for condition characteristics. Procedures for assigning condition attributes such as forest type, stand age, and stocking changed significantly with the introduction of the new annual plot design. However, FIA research (unpublished) comparing these plot designs, showed no noticeable difference in volume and tree-count estimates.

For additional information on the sample protocols and estimation procedures for the first two phases of the FIA program, see Bechtold and Patterson (2005). For additional information on Phase 3 indicator sampling protocols, see USDA Forest Service (2003) and Woodall and Monleon (2008).

QUALITY OF THE ESTIMATES

Two general types of error - random variability (precision) and estimation bias (accuracy) - are of interest to users. Random variability refers to the precision of the estimate, which would occur if the entire sampling and estimation process were repeated many times. Estimation bias refers to the difference between the estimate and the "true value" in the absence of this random variability, and to the overestimation or underestimation inherent in the entire estimation process.

Errors in the estimates in this report (both random variability and estimation bias) are affected by various sources. The four primary sources of error common to all sample-based estimates are sampling, measurement, prediction, and nonresponse error. The following sections provide a definition for each source of error in the context of the FIA inventory as well as a discussion of methods used to quantify and/or reduce that source of error. Measures of sampling, measurement, and prediction errors associated with various attributes are presented. Issues of possible bias related to nonresponse also are addressed.

Sampling Error

The process of sampling (selecting a random subset of a population and calculating estimates from this subset) causes estimates to contain error they would not have if every member of the population (e.g., every tree in Kansas) had been observed and included in the sample. The 2005 State inventory is based on a sample of 8,868 plots located randomly across Kansas (total area of 52.7 million acres), or a sampling rate of about one plot for every 5,937 acres.

The procedures for statistical estimation outlined in the previous section and described in detail in Bechtold and Patterson (2005) provide the estimates of the population totals and means in this report. Along with every estimate is an associated sampling error that is typically expressed as a percentage of the estimated value (the estimated value plus or minus the sampling error). This sampling error is the primary measure of the reliability of an estimate. We use a sampling error based on one standard error, that is, the chances are two in three that the results would have been within the limits indicated had a 100-percent inventory been conducted using these methods.

Sampling errors for State-level estimates of the major attributes presented in this report are in Table B. Table 65 presents includes errors for these estimates at the county-group level (counties assigned to each group are listed in the footnote).

Estimates for classifications smaller than the State totals in Table B have larger sampling errors. For example, Table 65 shows that the sampling error for timberland area in any county is higher than that for total timberland area in Kansas. To compute an approximate sampling error for an estimate that is smaller than a State total, use the following formula:

$$E = \frac{(SE)\sqrt{(\text{State total estimate})}}{\sqrt{(\text{Smaller estimate})}} \qquad (1)$$

where:

E = approximate sampling error for smaller estimate

SE = sampling error for State total estimate (percent)

For example, to compute the error on the area of forest land in the oak/hickory forest-type group for the State, proceed as follows:

The total area of the oak/hickory group in the State (from Table 3) is 1,267,800 acres.

The total area of all forest land in the State (from Table 3) is 2,105,500 acres.

The State total error for forest-land area (from Table B) is 3.74 percent.

Using formula (1):

Sampling error = $E = (3.74)\sqrt{2105500}\ /\sqrt{1267800} = 4.82$ percent.

This approximation works well for estimates of area, volume, number of trees, and biomass. Individuals seeking more accurate sampling errors should use the estimation tools available at http://fiatools.fs.fed.us.

The estimators used by FIA are unbiased under the assumptions that the sample plots are a random sample of the total population, and that the observed value for any plot is the true value for that plot. Deviations from these basic assumptions are not reflected in the computation of sampling errors. The following sections on measurement, prediction, and nonresponse error address possible departures from these basic assumptions.

Measurement Error

Errors associated with the methods and instruments used to observe and record the sample attributes are called measurement errors. On FIA plots, attributes such as the diameter and height of a tree are measured with different instruments; other attributes such as species and crown class are observed without the aid of an instrument. On a typical FIA plot, 15 to 50 trees are observed with 15 to 20 attributes recorded on each tree. Also, many attributes that describe the plot and conditions on the plot are observed. Errors in any of these observations affect the quality of the estimates. If a measurement is biased (such as tree diameter consistently taken at an incorrect place on the tree) the estimates that use this observation (such as volume) will reflect this bias. Even if measurements are unbiased, high levels of random error in the measurements will add to the total random error of the estimation process.

To ensure that all FIA observations are made to the highest standards possible, a regular program of quality control and quality assurance is an integral part of all FIA data-collection efforts. This program begins with the documentation of protocols and procedures used in the inventory followed by extensive crew training. To assess the quality of the data collected by these trained crews, a random sample of at least 4 percent of all plots is measured independently by a different qualified crew. These independent measurements are called blind checks. A second measurement on blind-check plots is made by a quality assurance (QA) crew. QA crews have as much or more experience and training in FIA field measurements as that of a standard FIA crew.

The quality of field measurements is assessed nationally through a set of measurement quality objectives (MQOs) that are set for every data item collected. Each MQO consists of two parts: a tolerance or acceptable level of measurement error and an objective in terms of the percentage of measurements within tolerance. Blind-check measurements are used to observe how often individual field crews are meeting these objectives and to assess the overall compliance among all crews. Table C shows the compliance rates for various measurements used to compute the estimates included in this and other FIA reports. The column labeled "Kansas" is based on blind-check measurements of plots used in this report. The column labeled "Plains States" includes all measurements by FIA crews within North Dakota, South Dakota, Nebraska, and Kansas. Data in the columns labeled "North Central States" were derived from measurements by FIA crews from 2000 through 2008 within an 11-state area (Illinois, Indiana, Iowa, Kansas, Michigan, Minnesota, Missouri, Nebraska, North Dakota, South Dakota, and Wisconsin). Training and supervision of crews is a regional effort and crews often work in more than one state. Regional data-quality observations reflect the overall measurement quality of all data collected by FIA in the Northern States.

In Kansas, variables such as d.b.h. have a low tolerance (± 0.1 inch) and a high percentage of data within the tolerance (82.1 percent). Measurements for determining tree-size class are precise. By contrast, variables such as stand age have a larger tolerance (± 10 years) and fewer data within the tolerance (64.3 percent). The estimate of stand age is based on the composition of all age classes within a stand. Often a stand is heterogeneous by age but a single value must be assigned to it. This can confound analysis of stand age over time.

Blind-check observations also were used to test for relative bias in the field-crew measurements. Relative bias is defined here as a tendency for standard measurements by field crews to be higher or lower than measurements by QA crews. The estimated relative bias and limits of 95-percent confidence intervals (based on parametric bootstrap estimates) for the relative bias are presented in Table D. Relative bias is reported only for variables that are measurements of continuous attributes (e.g., diameter and height) and several coded variables that are ordinal in nature (e.g., crown position). Relative bias is not appropriate for most coded variables.

Blind-check measurements do not provide direct observations of true bias in field measurements (average difference between field measurements and true values) because they are paired observations of two field measurements. The QA crew in these blind checks typically has more training and experience with FIA field measurements than the first crew, but both crews use the same methods and instruments to obtain measurements. These methods have been identified as the best available and selected for nationwide use by FIA, and are commonly used by similar natural-resource inventories. A basic assumption is that when applied correctly, these methods provide unbiased observations of the attribute they are designed to measure. Under this assumption, relative bias observations in Table D provide observations of bias due to the difference in experience and training between the field and QA crews. In most cases, there is no significant bias.

Prediction Error

Errors associated with mathematical models (such as volume models) aimed at providing observations of the attributes of interest based on sample attributes are called prediction errors. Area, number of trees, volume, biomass, growth, removals, and mortality are the primary attributes of interest in this report. Estimates of area and number of trees are based on direct observation and do not rely on prediction models. Models are used to predict volume and biomass estimates for individual trees. Change estimates such as growth, mortality, and removals are based on these model-based predictions of volume from both the current plot measurements and the measurements taken in the previous inventory.

Estimates of prediction errors associated with volume models used in this report are presented by Hahn and Hansen (1991) along with the model forms, methods used in model development, and model-parameter estimates. The estimated prediction errors are based on observations of 10,453 trees measured in the 1989 Missouri inventory (Spencer et al. 1992). For gross cubic-foot volume in live trees, there was a 2.5 percent overprediction across all species, an underprediction of 4.3 percent in trees less than 10 inches in d.b.h., and an overprediction of 7.1 in trees 20 inches and larger in d.b.h. Prediction errors were similar for board foot estimates.

In comparing FIA estimates with those from other data sources, users should be aware of the prediction models used in both estimates. If both estimates are based on the same prediction models with matching fitted-parameter values, the prediction bias of one estimate should cancel out that of the other estimate. If the estimates are based on different prediction models, the prediction error of both models must be considered.

Nonresponse Error

Nonresponse error occurs when crews are unable to measure a plot (or a portion of a plot) at a selected location. Nonresponse falls into three classes:

- Denied access – Entire plots or portions of plots where the field crew is unable to obtain permission from the landowner to measure trees on the plot.
- Hazardous/inaccessible – Entire plots or portions of plots where conditions prevent a crew from safely accessing the plot or measuring trees on the plot.
- Other – Plots on which the field crew is unable to obtain a valid measurement for reasons other than those stated.

Nonresponse has two effects on the sample: it reduces the sample size, which is reflected in the sampling errors, and it can bias the estimates if the portion of the population not being sampled differs from the portion being sampled.

In FIA, nonresponse rates are relatively low. In the 2005 Kansas inventory, 8,868 sample plots were selected for observation. All but 92 of these plots were included in the sample used to estimate current resources. On 90 plots, crews were unable to obtain owner permission to measure the plot or part of the plot; hazardous conditions on two plots prevented the crew from measuring all or part of the plot.

Even an overall nonresponse rate of 1 percent can cause considerable bias if not properly accounted for. The major source of nonresponse is denied access to plots, which occurs primarily on lands in private ownership. Also, observations for plots on nonforest land and water classes rarely require crews to physically enter the area, and permission is not needed because the observation can be obtained from aerial photos or other sources of remotely sensed information.

The stratified estimation process used by FIA with strata defined by two ownership classes (private and public) and four Landsat TM forest cover classes (nonforest, nonforest edge, forest edge, and forest) reduces the possible effects of bias caused by nonresponse. Under the stratified estimation process used by FIA, nonresponses are removed from the sample, and stratum estimates (means, totals, and sampling errors) are obtained only from plots with valid observations. The net effect in the estimates of means and totals is that the average of the observed plots within the stratum (ownership-forest-cover class) becomes the estimate for all nonresponses within that stratum. The nonresponse rate in one stratum does not affect the estimate in other strata. The response rate within each stratum for the Kansas 2005 inventory is presented in Table A.

In Table 1 of this report, we acknowledge denied access and hazardous as two land classes in Kansas within which we are unable to provide estimates for variables such as forest area and timber volume. However, we do report the total estimated area in each of these classes. In all other tables of this report, we do not acknowledge either of these classes, and in the estimation process we treat the sample where we do have observations as a random sample of the entire State.

The nonresponse plots in this inventory were not permanently removed from the FIA system of plots. We will attempt to measure these plots in future inventories. At that time we may be able to obtain permission to access these plots, hazardous conditions may have changed, and/or other circumstances that caused us to drop plots from a specific inventory cycle may well change.

GLOSSARY

Average annual mortality: The average annual change in mortality of trees during the period between inventories. This estimate can be provided in cubic feet for live and growing-stock trees that died or in board feet for sawtimber trees that died.

Average annual net growth: The average annual change in the volume of trees during the period between inventories. Components include the change in volume of trees that have met the minimum size requirements over the inventory period, plus the volume of trees reaching the minimum size during the period (ingrowth), minus the volume of trees that died during the period, minus the volume of cull during the period. Mortality removals (trees killed in the harvesting process and left on site) and diversion removals (trees removed from the forest-land base due to a change from forest to nonforest land) are not included. This estimate can be provided in cubic feet for live and growing-stock trees or in board feet for sawtimber trees.

Average annual removals: The average annual change in removals of trees during the period between inventories. The estimate includes harvest removals, mortality removals (trees killed in the harvesting process and left on site), and diversion removals (trees removed from the forest-land base due to a change from forest to nonforest land). This estimate can be provided in cubic feet for live and growing-stock trees or in board feet for sawtimber trees.

Basal area: Tree area in square feet of the cross section at breast height of a single tree. When the basal areas of all trees in a stand are summed, the result usually is expressed as square feet of basal area per acre.

Bioindicator species: A tree, woody shrub, or herb species that responds to ambient levels of ozone pollution with distinct visible foliar symptoms that are easy to diagnose.

Biomass: The aboveground volume of live trees (including bark but excluding foliage) reported in dry tons (dry weight). Biomass has four components:

Bole: Biomass of a tree from 1 foot above the ground to a 4-inch top outside bark or to a point where the central stem breaks into limbs.

Tops and limbs: Total biomass of a tree from a 1-foot stump minus the bole.

1- to 5-inch trees: Total aboveground biomass of a tree from 1 to 5 inches in d.b.h.

Stump: Biomass of a tree 5 inches d.b.h. and larger from the ground to a height of 1 foot.

Bulk density: The mass of soil per unit volume. A measure of the ratio of pore space to solid materials in a given soil. It is expressed in units of grams per cubic centimeter of oven dry soil.

Coarse woody debris (CWD): Dead branches, twigs, and wood splinters 3.0 inches in diameter and larger measured at the smallest end.

Commercial species: Tree species suitable for industrial wood products.

Compacted live crown ratio: The percent of the total length of the tree that supports a full, live crown. To determine compacted live crown ratio for trees that have uneven length crowns, lower branches are visually transferred to fill holes in the upper portions of the crown, until a full, even crown is created.

Corporate: An ownership class of private lands owned by corporations.

County and municipal: An ownership class of public lands owned by counties or local public agencies, or lands leased by these governmental units for more than 50 years. Also known as local government.

Cropland: Land under cultivation within the last 24 months, including cropland harvested, crop failures, cultivated summer fallow, idle cropland used only for pasture, orchards, active Christmas tree plantations indicated by annual shearing, nurseries, and land in soil improvement crops but excluding land cultivated in developing improved pasture.

Crown: The part of a tree or woody plant bearing live branches or foliage.

Crown dieback: Recent mortality of branches with fine twigs, which begins at the terminal portion of a branch and proceeds toward the trunk. Dieback is considered only when it occurs in the upper and outer portions of the tree. When whole branches are dead in the upper crown, without obvious signs of damage such as breaks or animal injury, it is assumed the branches died from the terminal portion of the branch. Dead branches in the lower portion of the live crown are assumed to have died from competition and shading.

Cull tree: A live tree, 5.0 inches in d.b.h. or larger, that is unmerchantable for saw logs now or prospectively because of rot, roughness, or species (see definitions for rotten and rough trees).

Decay class: Qualitative assessment of stage of decay (5 classes) of coarse woody debris based on visual assessments of color of wood, presence/absence of twigs and branches, texture of rotten portions, and structural integrity.

Diameter class: A classification of trees based on diameter outside bark measured at breast height (4-½ feet above ground). D.b.h. is the common abbreviation for "diameter at breast height." With 2-inch diameter classes, the 6-inch class, for example, includes trees 5.0 through 6.9 inches d.b.h. A "diameter at root collar" or d.r.c. measurement is acquired for multi-stemmed woodland species (e.g., Rocky Mountain juniper).

Down woody material (DWM): Woody pieces of trees and shrubs that have been uprooted (no longer supporting growth) or severed from their root system, not self-supporting, and lying on the ground.

Duff: A soil layer dominated by organic material derived from the decomposition of plant and animal litter and deposited on either an organic or a mineral surface. This layer is distinguished from the litter layer in that the original organic material has undergone sufficient decomposition that the source of this material (e.g., individual plant parts) no longer can be identified.

Effective cation exchange capacity (ECEC): The sum of cations that a soil can adsorb in its natural pH. It is expressed in units of centimoles of positive charge per kilogram of soil.

Federal: An ownership class of public lands owned by the U.S. Government.

Fiber products: Products derived from wood and bark residues, such as pulp, composition board products, and wood chips.

Fine materials: Wood residues not suitable for chipping, such as planer shavings and sawdust.

Fine woody debris (FWD): Dead branches, twigs, and wood splinters 0.1 to 2.9 inches in diameter.

Forest land: Land at least 10-percent stocked by trees of any size, including land that formerly had such tree cover and that will be naturally or artificially regenerated. Forest land includes transition zones, such as areas between heavily forested and nonforested lands that are at least 10-percent stocked with trees and forest areas adjacent to urban and builtup lands. Also included are pinyon-juniper and chaparral areas in the West and afforested areas. The minimum area for classification of forest land is 1 acre and 120 feet wide measured stem-to-stem from the outer-most edge. Unimproved roads and trails, streams, and clearings in forest areas are classified as forest if less than 120 feet wide.

Forest type: A classification of forest land based on the species presently forming a plurality of the live-tree stocking. If softwoods predominate (50 percent or more), then the forest type will be one of the softwood types and vice versa for hardwoods. For the Eastern United States, there are mixed hardwood-pine forest types when the pine and/or redcedar (either eastern or southern) component is between 25 and 49 percent of the stocking. If the pine/redcedar component is less than 25 percent of the stocking, then one of the hardwood forest types is assigned.

Forest-type group: Combinations of forest types that share closely associated species or site requirements and are generally combined for brevity of reporting.

Growing stock: A classification of timber inventory that includes live trees of commercial species meeting specified standards of quality or vigor. Rough and rotten cull trees are excluded. When associated with volume, this includes only trees 5.0 inches d.b.h. and larger.

Hardwood: A dicotyledonous tree, usually broad-leaved and deciduous.

    Soft hardwoods: A category of hardwood species with wood generally of low specific gravity (less than 0.5). Notable examples include hackberry, cottonwood, and American elm.

    Hard hardwoods: A category of hardwood species with wood generally of high specific gravity (greater than 0.5). Notable examples include green ash, Osage-orange, black walnut, and oaks.

Industrial wood: All commercial roundwood products except fuelwood.

Land area: The area of dry land and land temporarily or partly covered by water, such as marshes, swamps, and river flood plains; streams, sloughs, estuaries, and canals less than 200 feet wide; and lakes, reservoirs, and ponds less than 4.5 acres in area.

Litter: Undecomposed or only partially decomposed organic material that can be readily identified (e.g., plant leaves, twigs).

Live cull: A classification that includes live, cull trees. When associated with volume, it is the net volume in live, cull trees that are 5.0 inches d.b.h. and larger.

Local government: An ownership class of public lands owned by counties or local public agencies, or lands leased by these governmental units for more than 50 years. Also known as county and municipal.

Logging residues: The unused portions of growing-stock and nongrowing-stock trees cut or killed by logging and left in the woods.

Merchantable: Refers to a pulpwood or saw log section that meets pulpwood or saw log specifications, respectively.

National Forest: An ownership class of Federal lands, designated by executive order or statute as National Forests or purchase units, and other lands under the administration of the Forest Service, including experimental areas.

Net volume in cubic feet: The gross volume in cubic feet less deductions for rot, roughness, and poor form. Volume is computed for the central stem from a 1-foot stump to a minimum 4.0-inch top diameter outside bark, or to the point where the central stem breaks into limbs.

Noncommercial species: Tree species of typically small size, poor form, or inferior quality, which normally do not develop into trees suitable for industrial wood products.

Noncorporate private: Nongovernmental conservation and natural resource organizations; unincorporated local parternships, associations, and clubs; and Native American communities.

Nonforest land: Land that has never supported forests and lands formerly forested where use of timber management is precluded by development for other uses. (Note: Includes area used for crops, improved pasture, residential areas, city parks, improved roads of any width and adjoining clearings, powerline clearings of any width, and 1- to 4.5-acre areas of water classified by the Bureau of the Census as land. If intermingled in forest areas, unimproved roads and nonforest strips must be more than 120 feet wide, and clearings, etc., must be more than 1 acre in area to qualify as nonforest land.)

Nonstocked areas: Timberland less than 10-percent stocked with live trees.

Other red oaks: A group of species in the genus *Quercus* that includes scarlet oak, northern pin oak, southern red oak, bear oak, shingle oak, laurel oak, blackjack oak, water oak, pin oak, willow oak, and black oak.

Other white oaks: A group of species in the genus *Quercus* that includes overcup oak, chestnut oak, and post oak.

Ownership: The property owned by one ownership unit.

Ownership unit: A classification of ownership encompassing all types of legal entities having an ownership interest in land, regardless of the number of people involved. A unit may be an individual, a combination of persons; a legal entity such as a corporation, partnership, club, or trust, or a public agency. An ownership unit has control of a parcel or group of parcels of land.

Ozone: A regional, gaseous air pollutant produced primarily through sunlight-driven chemical reactions of nitrogen dioxide and hydrocarbons in the atmosphere and causing foliar injury to deciduous trees, conifers, shrubs, and herbaceous species.

Ozone bioindicator site: An open area used for ozone injury evaluations on ozone-sensitive species. The area must meet certain site selection guidelines on size, condition, and plant counts to be used for ozone injury evaluations in FIA.

Physiographic class: A measure of soil and water conditions that affect tree growth on a site. The physiographic classes are as follows:

Xeric: Very dry soils where excessive drainage seriously limits both growth and species occurrence. These sites are usually on upland and upper half slopes.

Xeromesic: Moderately dry soils where excessive drainage limits growth and species occurrence to some extent. These sites are usually on the lower half slopes.

Mesic: Deep, well-drained soils. Growth and species occurrence are limited only by climate. These include all cove sites (small sheltered bays) and bottomlands (low land) along intermittent streams.

Hydromesic: Moderately wet soils where insufficient drainage or infrequent flooding limits growth and species occurrence to some extent.

Hydric: Very wet sites where excess water seriously limits both growth and species occurrence.

Poletimber trees: Live trees at least 5.0 inches in d.b.h. but smaller than sawtimber trees.

Primary wood-using mill: A mill that converts roundwood products into other wood products. Common examples are sawmills that convert saw logs into lumber and pulpmills that convert pulpwood into wood pulp.

Productivity class: A classification of forest land in terms of potential annual cubic-foot volume growth per acre at culmination of mean annual increment in fully stocked natural stands.

Pulpwood: Roundwood, whole-tree chips, or wood residues used for the production of wood pulp.

Reserved forest land: Forest land withdrawn from timber utilization through statute, administrative regulation, or designation without regard to productive status.

Residues: Bark and woody materials that are generated in primary wood-using mills when roundwood products are converted to other products. Examples include slabs, edgings, trimmings, miscuts, sawdust, shavings, veneer cores and clippings, and pulp screenings. Includes bark residues and wood residues (both coarse and fine materials) but excludes logging residues.

Rotten tree: A live tree of commercial species that does not contain a saw log now or prospectively primarily because of rot (that is, when rot accounts for more than 50 percent of the total cull volume).

Rough tree: (a) A live tree of commercial species that does not contain a saw log now or prospectively primarily because of roughness (that is, when sound cull due to such factors as poor form, splits, or cracks accounts for more than 50 percent of the total cull volume) or (b) a live tree of noncommercial species.

Roundwood products: Logs, bolts, and other round timber generated from harvesting trees for industrial or consumer use.

Salvable dead tree: A downed or standing dead tree considered currently or potentially merchantable by regional standards.

Saplings: Live trees 1.0 inch through 4.9 inches d.b.h.

Saw log: A log meeting minimum standards of diameter, length, and defect, including logs at least 8 feet long, sound and straight, and with a minimum diameter inside bark of 6 inches for softwoods and 8 inches for hardwoods, or meeting other combinations of size and defect specified by regional standards.

Sawtimber tree: A live tree of commercial species containing at least a 12-foot saw log or two noncontiguous saw logs 8 feet or longer, and meeting regional specifications for freedom from defect. Softwoods must be at least 9.0 inches d.b.h. Hardwoods must be at least 11.0 inches d.b.h.

Sawtimber volume: Net volume of the saw-log portion of live sawtimber in board feet, International 1/4-inch rule (unless specified otherwise), from stump to a minimum 7.0 inches top d.o.b. for softwoods and a minimum 9.0 inches top d.o.b. for hardwoods.

Seedlings: Live trees less than 1.0 inch d.b.h. and at least 1 foot in height.

Select red oaks: A group of species in the genus *Quercus* that includes cherrybark oak, northern red oak, and Shumard oak.

Select white oaks: A group of species in the genus *Quercus* that includes white oak, swamp white oak, bur oak, swamp chestnut oak, and chinkapin oak.

Site index: An expression of forest site quality based on the height of a free-growing dominant or codominant tree of a representative species in the forest type at age 50.

Snag: A standing dead tree. In the current inventory, a snag must be 5.0 inches d.b.h./d.r.c. and 4.5 feet tall, and have a lean angle less than 45 degrees from vertical. A snag may be either self-supported by its roots, or supported by another tree or snag.

Softwood: A coniferous tree, usually evergreen, having needles or scale-like leaves.

Soil Order: The broadest category or class of soil based largely on the processes that formed the soil as indicated by the presence or absence of diagnostic horizons or layers.

Sound dead: The net volume in salvable dead trees.

Stand: A group of trees on a minimum of 1 acre of forest land that is stocked by forest trees of any size.

Stand-size class: A classification of forest land based on the size class of live trees in the area. The classes are as follows:

> *Nonstocked:* Forest land stocked with less than 10 percent of full stocking with live trees. Examples are recently cutover areas or recently reverted agricultural fields.
>
> *Seedling-sapling:* Forest land stocked with at least 10 percent of full stocking with live trees with half or more of such stocking in seedlings or saplings or both.
>
> *Poletimber:* Forest land stocked with at least 10 percent of full stocking with live trees with half or more of such stocking in poletimber or sawtimber trees or both, and in which the stocking of poletimber exceeds that of sawtimber.
>
> *Sawtimber:* Forest land stocked with at least 10 percent of full stocking with live trees with half or more of such stocking in poletimber or sawtimber trees or both, and in which the stocking of sawtimber is at least equal to that of poletimber.

State: An ownership class of public lands owned by states or lands leased by states for more than 50 years. Also a general reference to one of the political and geographic subdivisions of the United States.

Stocking: The degree of occupancy of land by trees, measured by basal area or number of trees by size and spacing, or both, compared to a stocking standard; that is, the basal area or number of trees, or both, required to fully utilize the growth potential of the land.

Timberland: Forest land that is producing or is capable of producing crops of industrial wood and not withdrawn from timber utilization by statute or administrative regulation. (Note: Areas qualifying as timberland are capable of producing in excess of 20 cubic feet per acre per year of industrial wood in natural stands. Currently inaccessible and inoperable areas are included.)

Timber products output: All timber products cut from roundwood and byproducts of wood manufacturing plants. Roundwood products include logs, bolts, or other round sections cut from growing-stock trees, cull trees, salvable dead trees, trees on nonforest land, noncommercial species, sapling-size trees, and limbwood. Byproducts from primary manufacturing plants include slabs, edging, trimmings, miscuts, sawdust, shavings, veneer cores and clippings, and screenings of pulpmills that are used as pulpwood chips or other products.

Tree: A woody plant usually having one or more erect perennial stems, a stem diameter at breast height of at least 3.0 inches, a more or less definitely formed crown of foliage, and a height of at least 15 feet at maturity.

Tree size class: A classification of trees based on diameter at breast height, including sawtimber trees, poletimber trees, saplings, and seedlings.

Tops: The wood of a tree above the merchantable height (or above the point on the stem 4.0 inches diameter outside bark (d.o.b.) or to the point where the central stem breaks into limbs). It includes the usable material in the uppermost stem.

Urban forest land: Land that would otherwise meet the criteria for timberland but is in an urban-suburban area surrounded by commercial, industrial, or residential development and not likely to be managed for the production of industrial wood products on a continuing basis. Wood removed would be for land clearing, fuelwood, or esthetic purposes. Such forest land may be associated with industrial, commercial, residential subdivision, industrial parks, golf course perimeters, airport buffer strips, and public urban parks that qualify as forest land.

Unreserved forest land: Forest land not withdrawn from harvest by statute or administrative regulation. This includes forest lands that are not capable of producing in excess of 20 cubic feet per acre per year of industrial wood in natural stands.

Veneer log: A roundwood product from which veneer is sliced or sawn and that usually meets certain standards of minimum diameter and length and maximum defect.

Weight: The weight of wood and bark, oven-dry basis (approximately 12 percent moisture content).

LITERATURE CITED

Bechtold, W.A.; Patterson, P.L., eds. 2005. **The enhanced Forest Inventory and Analysis program—national sampling design and estimation procedures.** Gen. Tech. Rep. SRS-80. Asheville, NC: U.S. Department of Agriculture, Forest Service, Southern Research Station. 85 p.

Chase, C.D.; Strickler, J.K. 1968. **Kansas woodlands.** Resour. Bull. NC-4. St. Paul, MN: U.S. Department of Agriculture, Forest Service, North Central Forest Experiment Station. 50 p.

DellaSala, D.A.; Staus, N.L.; Strittholt, J.R.; Hackman, A.; Iacobelli, A. 2001. **An updated protected areas database for the United States and Canada.** Natural Areas Journal. 21(2): 124-135.

Hahn, J.T.; Hansen, M.H. 1991. **Cubic and board foot volume models for the Central States.** Northern Journal of Applied Forestry. 8: 47-57.

Hansen, M.H.; Wendt, D.G. 2000. **Using classified Landsat Thematic Mapper data for stratification in a statewide forest inventory.** In: McRoberts, R.E.; Reams, G.A.; Van Deusen, P.C., eds. Proceedings of the first annual Forest Inventory and Analysis symposium. Gen. Tech. Rep. NC-213. St. Paul, MN: U.S. Department of Agriculture, Forest Service, North Central Research Station.

Leatherberry, E.C.; Schmidt, T.L.; Strickler, J.K.; Aslin, R.G. 1999. **An analysis of the forest resources of Kansas, 1994.** Res. Pap. NC-334. St. Paul, MN: U.S. Department of Agriculture, Forest Service, North Central Research Station. 114 p.

McRoberts, R.E. 1999. **Joint annual forest inventory and monitoring system: the North Central perspective.** Journal of Forestry. 97: 21-26.

McRoberts, R.E.; Wendt, D.G.; Nelson, M.D.; Hansen, M.H. 2002. **Using a land cover classification based on satellite imagery to improve the precision of forest inventory area estimates.** Remote Sensing of the Environment. 80: 1-9.

McRoberts, R.E. 2005. **The enhanced forest inventory and analysis program.** In: Bechtold, W.A.; Patterson, P. L., eds. The enhanced forest inventory and analysis program—national sampling design and estimation procedures. Gen. Tech. Rep. SRS-80. Asheville, NC: U.S. Department of Agriculture, Forest Service, Southern Research Station: 1-10.

Montreal Process. 1995. **Criteria and indicators for the conservation and sustainable management of temperate and boreal forests.** Hull, QC: Canadian Forest Service. 27 p.

Moser, W. Keith; Hansen, Mark H.; Atchison, Robert L.;, Brand, Gary J.; Butler, Brett J.; Crocker, Susan J.; Meneguzzo, Dacia M.; Nelson, Mark D.; Perry, Charles H.; Reading, William H. IV; Wilson, Barry T.; Woodall, Christopher W. 2008. **Kansas forests 2005.** Resour. Bull. NRS-26. Newtown Square, PA: U.S. Department of Agriculture, Forest Service, Northern Research Station. 125 p.

Spencer, J.S., Jr.; Strickler, J.K.; Moyer, W.J. 1984. **Kansas forest inventory, 1981.** Resour. Bull. NC-83. St. Paul, MN: U.S. Department of Agriculture, Forest Service, North Central Forest Experiment Station. 134 p.

Spencer, J.S., Jr.; Roussopoulos, S.M.; Massengale, R.A. 1992. **Missouri's forest resource, 1989: an analysis.** Resour. Bull. NC-139. St. Paul, MN: U.S. Department of Agriculture, Forest Service, North Central Forest Experiment Station. 84 p.

USDA Forest Service. 2003. **Forest inventory and analysis national core field guide; Volume I: field data collection procedures for phase 2 plots, Volume II: Field data collection procedures for phase 3 plots. Version 2.0.** St. Paul, MN: U.S. Department of Agriculture, Forest Service, North Central Research Station. 410 p.

Vogelmann, J.E.; Howard, S.M.; Yang, L.; Larson, C.R.; Wylie, B.K.; Van Driel, N. 2001. **Completion of the 1990s National Land Cover Data Set for the conterminous United States from Landsat Thematic Mapper data and ancillary data sources.** Photogrammetric Engineering and Remote Sensing. 67: 650-662.

Woodall, C.W.; Monleon, V.J. 2008. **Sampling protocol, estimation, and analysis procedures for the down woody materials indicator of the FIA program.** Gen. Tech. Rep. NRS-22. Newtown Square, PA: U.S. Department of Agriculture, Forest Service, Northern Research Station. 68 p.

TABLES OF QUALITY ASSURANCE

Table A.—Area and number of plots in each stratum, Kansas, 2001-2005

Table B.—State-level estimates of major forest-resource attributes and their sampling errors, Kansas, 2001-2005

Table C.—Measurement quality objective (MQO) tolerance compliance based on blind-check plots, Kansas, 2001-2005

Table D.—Observed relative bias values (Average [field crew - QA crew]) for measurement variables on blind check plots, Kansas, 2001-2005

TABLES OF ESTIMATION

Gaps in the enumeration of tables are placeholders for future reports.

Area

Table 1.—Percentage of area by land status, Kansas, 2001-2005

Table 2.—Area of forest land, in thousand acres, by owner class and forest-land status, Kansas, 2001-2005

Table 3.—Area of forest land, in thousand acres, by forest-type group and productivity class, Kansas, 2001-2005

Table 4.—Area of forest land, in thousand acres, by forest-type group, ownership group, and forest-land status, Kansas, 2001-2005

Table 5.—Area of forest land, in thousand acres, by forest-type group and stand-size class, Kansas, 2001-2005

Table 6.—Area of forest land, in thousand acres, by forest-type group and stand-age class, Kansas, 2001-2005

Table 7.—Area of forest land, in thousand acres, by forest-type group and stand origin, Kansas, 2001-2005

Table 8.—Area of forest land, in thousand acres, by forest-type group and disturbance class, Kansas, 2001-2005

Table 9.—Area of timberland, in thousand acres, by forest-type group and stand-size class, Kansas, 2001-2005

Number

Table 10.—Number of live trees (at least 1 inch d.b.h./d.r.c.), in thousand trees, on forest land by species group and diameter class, Kansas, 2001-2005

Table 11.—Number of growing-stock trees (at least 5 inches d.b.h.), in thousand trees, on timberland by species group and diameter class, Kansas, 2001-2005

Table 11a.—Number of growing-stock trees, in thousands, on timberland by species and diameter class, Kansas, 2001-2005

Volume

Table 12.—Net volume of live trees (at least 5 inches d.b.h./d.r.c.), in million cubic feet, by owner class and forest-land status, Kansas, 2001-2005

Table 13.—Net volume of live trees (at least 5 inches d.b.h./d.r.c.), in million cubic feet, on forest land by forest-type group and stand-size class, Kansas, 2001-2005

Table 13a.—Net volume of all live trees, in million cubic feet, on forest land by species and forest type group, Kansas, 2001-2005

Table 14.—Net volume of live trees (at least 5 inches d.b.h./d.r.c.), in million cubic feet, on forest land by species group and ownership group, Kansas, 2001-2005

Table 15.—Net volume of live trees (at least 5 inches d.b.h./d.r.c.), in million cubic feet, on forest land by species group and diameter class, Kansas, 2001-2005

Table 15a.—Net volume of all live trees, in million cubic feet, on forest land by species and diameter class, Kansas, 2001-2005

Table 16.—Net volume of live trees (at least 5 inches d.b.h./d.r.c.), in million cubic feet, on forest land by forest-type group and stand origin, Kansas, 2001-2005

Table 17.—Net volume of growing-stock trees (at least 5 inches d.b.h.), in million cubic feet, on timberland by species group and diameter class, Kansas, 2001-2005

Table 17a.—Net volume of growing-stock trees, in million cubic feet, on timberland by species and diameter class, Kansas, 2001-2005

Table 18.—Net volume of growing-stock trees (at least 5 inches d.b.h.), in million cubic feet, on timberland by species group and ownership group, Kansas, 2001-2005

Table 19.—Net volume of sawtimber trees (International 1/4-inch rule), in million board feet, on timberland by species group and diameter class, Kansas, 2001-2005

Table 19a.—Net volume of sawtimber trees (Doyle rule), in million board feet, on timberland by species group and diameter class, Kansas, 2001-2005

Table 20.—Net volume of saw-log portion of sawtimber trees, in million cubic feet, on timberland by species group and ownership group, Kansas, 2001-2005

Weight

Table 31.—Aboveground dry weight of live trees (at least 1 inch d.b.h./d.r.c.), in thousand dry short tons, by owner class and forest-land status, Kansas, 2001-2005

Table 32.—Aboveground dry weight of live trees (at least 1 inch d.b.h./d.r.c.), in thousand dry short tons, on forest land by species group and diameter class, Kansas, 2001-2005

County-Level

Table 54.—Area of forest land, in thousand acres, by inventory unit, county, and forest-land status, Kansas, 2001-2005

Table 55.—Area of forest land, in thousand acres, by inventory unit, county, ownership group, and forest-land status, Kansas, 2001-2005

Table 56.—Area of forest land, in thousand acres, by county group, and forest type group, Kansas 2001-2005

Table 57.—Area of timberland, in thousand acres, by inventory unit, county, and stand-size class, Kansas, 2001-2005

Table 58.—Area of timberland, in thousand acres, by inventory unit, county, and stocking class, Kansas, 2001-2005

Table 59.—Net volume of growing-stock trees (at least 5 inches d.b.h.), in million cubic feet, and sawtimber trees (International 1/4-inch rule), in million board feet, on timberland by inventory unit, county, and major species group, Kansas, 2001-2005

Table 59a.—Net volume of growing-stock trees (at least 5 inches d.b.h.), in million cubic feet, and sawtimber trees (Doyle rule), in million board feet, on timberland by inventory unit, county, and major species group, Kansas, 2001-2005

Table 65.—Sampling errors by Forest Survey Unit/County group for area of forestland, area of timberland, growing-stock volume on timberland, and sawtimber volume on timberland, Kansas, 2001-2005

Table A.—Area and number of plots in each stratum, Kansas, 2001-2005

Forest survey unit[a]	Ownership layer[b]	Classified NLCD layer[c]	Area[d] (acres)	Selected[e]	Nonforest office plots[f]	Field check plots[g]	Field check plots measured[h]	Forest plots measured[i]	Denied access	Hazardous
1	Private	Forest	137,441	14	0	14	14	14	0	0
1	Private	Forest edge	554,826	113	28	85	76	73	9	1
1	Private	Nonforest	6,598,304	1,125	1,041	84	78	53	7	0
1	Private	Nonforest edge	1,150,785	170	91	79	70	60	9	0
2	Private	Forest	203,555	30	3	27	23	23	4	0
2	Private	Forest edge	660,325	89	32	57	50	46	7	0
2	Private	Nonforest	7,606,283	1,260	1,202	58	47	29	11	0
2	Private	Nonforest edge	1,382,629	278	183	95	82	71	14	0
3	Private	Forest and forest edge	315,857	59	25	34	31	26	3	0
3	Private	Nonforest	32,799,497	5,518	5,437	81	66	41	14	1
3	Private	Nonforest edge	940,479	158	110	48	38	27	12	0
Total private			52,349,981	8,814	8,152	662	575	463	90	2
1	Public	All	108,251	17	14	3	3	3	0	0
2	Public	All	38,102	9	6	3	3	2	0	0
3	Public	All	160,948	28	28	0	0	0	0	0
Total public			307,301	54	48	6	6	5	0	0
State total			52,657,282	8,868	8,200	668	581	468	90	2

[a] Forest survey unit—1 = Northeastern, 2 = Southeastern, 3 = Western.

[b] Ownership layer—Classification based on Protected Areas Database.

[c] Classified NLCD layer—Classification based on the 1992 NLCD classification and 2-pixel edge zones.

[d] Total area defined by intersection of ownership and classified NLCD layers within group of counties specified.

[e] Selected—Total number of plots selected to be sampled.

[f] Nonforest office plots—Selected plots whose observed classification as nonforest based on examination of aerial photographs and/or digital orthoquads.

[g] Field check plots—Selected plots that required field measurement.

[h] Field check plots measured—Field check plots where measurement was completed successfully. Excludes plots that were denied access, hazardous, or lost and measurement was not possible.

[i] Forest plots measured—Field check plots where forest condition was present on plot and measurement was completed in 2004 inventory. These plots are used to estimate current conditions, e.g., area, volume, number of trees, and biomass.

Table B.—State-level estimates of major forest-resource attributes and their sampling errors, Kansas, 2001-2005

Item	State total	Sampling error
	thousand cubic feet	*percent*
Growing stock on timberland		
Volume	1,457	7.86
Sawtimber on timberland	*thousand board feet[a]*	
Volume	5,356	9.63
Area:	*acres*	
Forest land	2,105,502	3.74
Timberland	2,027,679	3.87
Biomass (aboveground live trees)	*thousand dry tons*	
Forest land	73,001	5.10
Timberland	70,819	5.24

[a] International ¼-inch rule.

26

Table C.—Measurement quality objective (MQO) tolerance compliance based on blind-check plots, Kansas, 2001-2005

Variable	Tolerance	Kansas			Plains States		North Central States	
		Objective	Data within tolerance	Records	Data within tolerance	Records	Data within tolerance	Records
Plot Level								
National Variables								
Distance to Road	No Tolerance	90.0%	75.9%	29	69.4%	85	82.0%	1,677
Water on Plot	No Tolerance	90.0%	65.5%	29	85.9%	85	87.8%	1,677
Regional Variables								
ELEVATION_GPS	±50 ft	99.0%	66.7%	27	72.2%	79	83.0%	1,528
LAT_DECIMAL_DEG	±0.0001 dg	99.0%	96.4%	28	93.8%	81	92.0%	1,538
LON_DECIMAL_DEG	±0.0001 dg	99.0%	100.0%	28	93.8%	81	90.6%	1,538
LAT_FEET	±140 ft		100.0%	28	98.8%	81	98.6%	1,538
LON_FEET	±140 ft		100.0%	28	97.5%	81	97.7%	1,538
Results for:				29 Plots		85 Plots		1,677 Plots
Condition Level								
National Variables								
Condition Status	No Tolerance	99.0%	97.3%	74	98.2%	217	99.0%	2,595
Reserve Status	No Tolerance	99.0%	98.6%	74	98.6%	217	99.4%	2,595
Owner Group	No Tolerance	99.0%	89.3%	28	92.0%	75	98.2%	1,810
Forest Type (Type)	No Tolerance	95.0%	46.4%	28	70.7%	75	82.7%	1,810
Forest Type (Group)	No Tolerance	99.0%	64.3%	28	82.7%	75	90.4%	1,810
Stand Size	No Tolerance	99.0%	64.3%	28	73.3%	75	87.0%	1,810
Regeneration Status	No Tolerance	99.0%	96.4%	28	98.7%	75	98.6%	1,810
Tree Density	No Tolerance	99.0%	85.7%	28	92.0%	75	96.9%	1,810
Owner Class	No Tolerance	99.0%	85.7%	28	88.0%	75	95.6%	1,810
Owner Status	No Tolerance	99.0%	100.0%	28	100.0%	75	98.0%	1,810
Regeneration Species	No Tolerance	99.0%	96.4%	28	98.7%	75	98.4%	1,810
Stand Age	±10 %	95.0%	64.3%	28	50.7%	75	68.1%	1,810
Disturbance 1	No Tolerance	99.0%	65.4%	26	76.7%	73	93.1%	1,796
Disturbance Year 1	±1 yr	99.0%	60.0%	5	62.5%	16	74.2%	62
Disturbance 2	No Tolerance	99.0%	85.7%	14	82.1%	28	93.1%	175
Disturbance Year 2	±1 yr	99.0%	100.0%	1	50.0%	2	33.3%	3
Disturbance 3	No Tolerance	99.0%	100.0%	2	100.0%	6	92.9%	14
Disturbance Year 3	±1 yr	99.0%		.		.		
Treatment 1	No Tolerance	99.0%	92.3%	26	86.3%	73	95.2%	1,796

27

Table D.—Observed relative bias values (Average [field crew - QA crew]) for measurement variables on blind check plots, Kansas, 2001-2005

Variable	Units of measure	Kansas Relative bias	Kansas 95% CI Lower	Kansas 95% CI Upper	Kansas Number of observations	Plains States Relative bias	Plains 95% CI Lower	Plains 95% CI Upper	Plains Number of observations	North Central States Relative bias	NC 95% CI Lower	NC 95% CI Upper	NC Number of observations
Plot Level													
National Variables													
Distance to Road	code	-0.21	-0.66	0.10	29	-0.15	-0.42	0.13	85	-0.02	-0.07	0.03	1,677
Regional Variables													
ELEVATION_GPS	feet	-18.22	-37.04	-3.44	27	-27.20	-52.73	-8.78	79	-23.61	-51.95	-1.69	1,528
LAT_DECIMAL_DEG	degree	0.00	0.00	0.00	28	0.00	0.00	0.00	81	0.00	-0.01	0.00	1,538
LON_DECIMAL_DEG	degree	0.00	0.00	0.00	28	0.00	0.00	0.00	81	0.55	0.00	1.64	1,538
LAT_FEET	feet	5.21	-2.71	14.75	28	9.67	-4.27	32.40	81	-1,389.31	-3,933.65	-0.09	1,538
LON_FEET	feet	-7.44	-19.20	2.51	28	-43.51	-137.66	8.44	81	8,198.92	107.96	24,710.51	1,538
Results for:					**29 Plots**				**85 Plots**				**1,677 Plots**
Condition Level													
National Variables													
Stand Size	code	0.04	-0.25	0.32	28	0.03	-0.13	0.17	75	0.01	-0.01	0.02	1,810
Stand Age	years	-0.50	-3.36	2.45	28	-1.39	-4.88	1.95	75	-0.72	-1.28	-0.24	1,810
Results for:					**74 Conditions**				**217 Conditions**				**2,595 Conditions**
Subplot Level													
National Variables													
Slope	percent	-0.13	-1.05	0.96	112	-0.23	-1.55	0.97	328	0.63	0.16	1.21	6,535
Aspect	degrees	-10.81	-26.53	5.56	94	-8.36	-18.23	-0.41	287	-0.57	-1.79	0.74	6,021
Snow/Water Depth	feet	-0.79	-1.96	0.07	112	-0.05	-0.46	0.27	328	-0.40	-0.55	-0.25	6,535
Results for:					**112 Subplots**				**328 Subplots**				**6,535 Subplots**
Tree Level													
National Variables													
DBH	inches	-0.10	-0.20	-0.03	340	-0.09	-0.16	-0.04	945	-0.02	-0.03	-0.02	27,896
DRC	inches					0.11	-0.15	0.43	27	0.11	-0.15	0.43	27
Rotten/Missing Cull	percent	-0.11	-0.93	0.68	309	-0.35	-0.76	0.09	813	0.02	-0.04	0.07	18,782
Total Length	feet	1.48	0.03	2.88	310	1.68	0.63	2.50	789	0.30	0.08	0.52	17,997
Actual Length	feet	-19.40	-65.49	6.41	25	-8.82	-25.30	1.11	79	-1.37	-2.32	-0.54	1,973
Compacted Crown Ratio	percent	1.14	0.12	2.16	319	1.04	0.27	1.91	888	0.33	0.20	0.47	24,377
Uncompacted Crown Ratio (P3)	percent	-27.41	-36.85	-16.67	27	-27.11	-34.00	-19.08	75	-3.32	-4.29	-2.26	1,061
Crown position	code	-1.07	-1.44	-0.65	27	-0.97	-1.21	-0.73	75	-0.16	-0.20	-0.12	850
Crown light exposure	code	-0.78	-1.19	-0.39	27	-0.83	-1.09	-0.57	75	-0.12	-0.17	-0.06	1,061
Sapling crown vigor class	code									-0.11	-0.19	-0.05	211
Crown density	percent	-25.19	-34.26	-16.39	27	-26.40	-32.63	-20.07	75	-3.04	-4.29	-2.06	850
Crown dieback	percent	-4.26	-11.02	1.39	27	-1.27	-3.90	0.90	75	-0.34	-0.90	0.12	850
Transparency	percent	-16.85	-24.44	-8.52	27	-15.00	-18.67	-11.43	75	-1.76	-2.61	-1.06	850
Regional Variables													
NC Tree Class	code	0.04	-0.31	0.40	340	0.12	-0.16	0.34	971	0.05	0.01	0.10	27,083
DBH-live & decay code 1-2 trees	inches	-0.11	-0.20	-0.02	325	-0.09	-0.15	-0.03	892	-0.03	-0.04	-0.02	25,185
DBH-decay code 3-4-5 trees	inches	-0.03	-0.10	0.02	15	-0.31	-0.70	-0.04	36	-0.03	-0.06	-0.01	1,133
Total length trees 40 ft plus	feet	1.77	-0.01	3.48	171	2.42	1.52	3.43	459	0.75	0.60	0.87	14,813
Total length trees less than 40 ft	feet	1.13	-1.05	3.17	139	0.65	-1.30	2.13	330	-1.79	-2.83	-0.84	3,184
Total Length trees lt 5 inch	feet					13.40	8.42	19.80	25	2.39	0.53	4.43	230
Results for:					**340 Trees**				**972 Trees**				**27,923 Trees**
Seedling Level													
National Variables													

(Table D continued on next page)

(Table D continued)

Variable	Units of measure	Kansas				Plains States				North Central States			
		Relative bias	95% CI limits Lower	Upper	Number of observations	Relative bias	95% CI limits Lower	Upper	Number of observations	Relative bias	95% CI limits Lower	Upper	Number of observations
Seedling Count	number	-49.30	-77.86	-26.50	62	-40.39	-64.46	-18.12	127	-12.04	-15.05	-9.61	5,659
Seedling Count coded	number	-0.52	-0.85	-0.19	62	-0.34	-0.56	-0.10	127	0.02	0.00	0.04	5,659
Results for:	**Results for:**				**31 Microplots**				**80 Microplots**				**2,402 Microplots**
Site Tree Level													
National Variables													
Diameter	inches	-0.06	-0.10	-0.03	28	-0.15	-0.37	-0.04	94	-0.01	-0.02	0.01	2,870
Species	code	0.00	0.00	0.00	28	0.01	0.00	0.03	94	-0.15	-0.37	0.01	3,003
Total_length	feet	2.09	-0.13	4.57	28	0.80	-1.85	2.67	94	0.26	0.01	0.53	2,870
Diameter_age	years	0.29	-1.36	1.95	28	-1.45	-3.16	0.29	94	0.15	-0.05	0.34	2,870
Regional Variables													
Field_site_index	feet	0.00	0.00	0.00	28	0.00	0.00	0.00	94	0.09	0.01	0.19	3,003
Results for:	**Results for:**				**28 SI Trees**				**94 SI Trees**				**3,003 SI Trees**

Table 1.— Percentage of area by land status, Kansas, 2001-2005

Land status	Percentage of area
Accessible forest land	
Unreserved forest land	
Timberland	3.6
Unproductive	0.1
Total unreserved forest land	3.8
Reserved forest land	
Productive	0.0
Unproductive	- -
Total reserved forest land	0.0
All accessible forest land	3.8
Nonforest and other land	
Nonforest land	94.7
Water	
Census	0.3
Non-Census	0.2
All nonforest and other land	95.2
Nonsampled land	
Access denied	1.0
Hazardous conditions	0.0
Other	- -
All land	100.0

Total area (thousands of acres) 52,657

All table cells without observations in the inventory sample are indicated by --. Table value of 0.0 indicates the percentage rounds to less than 0.1 percent. Columns and rows may not add to their totals due to rounding.

Table 2.—Area of forest land, in thousand acres, by owner class and forest-land status, Kansas, 2001-2005

Owner class	Unreserved forests			Reserved forests			All forest land
	Timberland	Unproductive	Total	Productive	Unproductive	Total	
Other Federal							
Fish and Wildlife Service	4.7	--	4.7	--	--	--	4.7
Department of Defense or Energy	43.3	--	43.3	--	--	--	43.3
Other Federal	24.8	--	24.8	--	--	--	24.8
State and local government							
State	18.3	1.3	19.6	--	--	--	19.6
Local (county, municipal, etc.)	17.6	--	17.6	1.5	1.5	1.5	19.1
Private							
Undifferentiated private	1,918.9	75.0	1,994.0	--	--	--	1,994.0
All owners	2,027.7	76.3	2,104.0	1.5	1.5	1.5	2,105.5

All table cells without observations in the inventory sample are indicated by --. Table value of 0.0 indicates the acres round to less than 0.1 thousand acres. Columns and rows may not add to their totals due to rounding.

Table 3.—Area of forest land, in thousand acres, by forest-type group and productivity class, Kansas, 2001-2005

Forest-type group	Site productivity class (cubic feet/acre/year)							All classes
	0-19	20-49	50-84	85-119	120-164	165-224	225+	
White / red / jack pine group	--	--	--	--	3.1	--	--	3.1
Other eastern softwoods group	5.1	74.3	5.5	--	--	--	--	85.0
Ponderosa pine group	--	--	--	7.1	--	--	--	7.1
Oak / pine group	--	32.0	19.3	--	--	--	--	51.3
Oak / hickory group	64.9	677.7	385.1	123.4	12.7	4.0	--	1,267.8
Oak / gum / cypress group	--	--	--	6.5	--	--	--	6.5
Elm / ash / cottonwood group	1.6	231.6	219.6	118.4	17.3	0.9	--	589.3
Maple / beech / birch group	--	7.6	--	--	8.1	--	--	15.7
Other hardwoods group	4.7	13.9	3.9	--	--	--	--	22.5
Exotic hardwoods group	--	26.4	1.5	--	--	--	--	27.9
Nonstocked	--	25.9	3.5	--	--	--	--	29.4
All forest-type groups	76.3	1,089.3	638.4	255.5	41.1	4.9	--	2,105.5

All table cells without observations in the inventory sample are indicated by --. Table value of 0.0 indicates the acres round to less than 0.1 thousand acres. Columns and rows may not add to their totals due to rounding.

Table 4.— Area of forest land, in thousand acres, by forest-type group, ownership group, and forest-land status, Kansas, 2001-2005

Forest-type group	Forest Service		Other Federal		State and local government		Undifferentiated private		All forest land
	Timber-land	Other forest land	Timber-land	Other forest land	Timber-land	Other forest land	Timber-land	Other forest land	
White / red / jack pine group	--	--	3.1	--	--	--	--	--	3.1
Other eastern softwoods group	--	--	--	--	--	1.3	79.8	3.8	85.0
Ponderosa pine group	--	--	7.1	--	--	--	--	--	7.1
Oak / pine group	--	--	--	--	--	--	51.3	--	51.3
Oak / hickory group	--	--	30.3	--	20.9	--	1,151.7	64.9	1,267.8
Oak / gum / cypress group	--	--	--	--	--	--	6.5	--	6.5
Elm / ash / cottonwood group	--	--	26.0	--	15.0	--	546.7	1.6	589.3
Maple / beech / birch group	--	--	--	--	--	--	15.7	--	15.7
Other hardwoods group	--	--	4.5	--	--	--	13.3	4.7	22.5
Exotic hardwoods group	--	--	--	--	--	1.5	26.4	--	27.9
Nonstocked	--	--	1.9	--	--	--	27.5	--	29.4
All forest-type groups	--	--	72.8	--	35.9	2.8	1,918.9	75.0	2,105.5

All table cells without observations in the inventory sample are indicated by --. Table value of 0.0 indicates the acres round to less than 0.1 thousand acres. Columns and rows may not add to their totals due to rounding.

33

Table 5.— Area of forest land, in thousand acres, by forest-type group and stand-size class, Kansas, 2001-2005

Forest-type group	Stand-size class					All size classes
	Large diameter	Medium diameter	Small diameter	Chaparral	Nonstocked	
White / red / jack pine group	3.1	--	--	--	--	3.1
Other eastern softwoods group	14.3	22.5	48.1	--	--	85.0
Ponderosa pine group	--	7.1	--	--	--	7.1
Oak / pine group	17.4	19.8	14.1	--	--	51.3
Oak / hickory group	467.9	593.2	206.7	--	--	1,267.8
Oak / gum / cypress group	--	6.5	--	--	--	6.5
Elm / ash / cottonwood group	450.8	99.6	38.9	--	--	589.3
Maple / beech / birch group	7.6	8.1	--	--	--	15.7
Other hardwoods group	6.0	6.1	10.4	--	--	22.5
Exotic hardwoods group	9.1	12.4	6.4	--	--	27.9
Nonstocked	--	--	--	--	29.4	29.4
All forest-type groups	**976.3**	**775.3**	**324.5**	**--**	**29.4**	**2,105.5**

All table cells without observations in the inventory sample are indicated by --. Table value of 0.0 indicates the acres round to less than 0.1 thousand acres. Columns and rows may not add to their totals due to rounding.

Table 6.—Area of forest land, in thousand acres, by forest-type group and stand-age class, Kansas, 2001-2005

Forest-type group	Non stocked	Stand-age class (years)											All classes
		1-20	21-40	41-60	61-80	81-100	101-120	121-140	141-160	161-180	181-200	201+	
White / red / jack pine group	--	--	3.1	--	--	--	--	--	--	--	--	--	3.1
Other eastern softwoods group	--	15.9	50.2	16.1	2.8	--	--	--	--	--	--	--	85.0
Ponderosa pine group	--	--	7.1	--	--	--	--	--	--	--	--	--	7.1
Oak / pine group	--	12.6	24.2	10.1	4.5	--	--	--	--	--	--	--	51.3
Oak / hickory group	--	122.7	574.4	379.6	136.4	53.3	1.3	--	--	--	--	--	1,267.8
Oak / gum / cypress group	--	--	1.3	5.2	--	--	--	--	--	--	--	--	6.5
Elm / ash / cottonwood group	--	33.8	262.3	243.7	38.6	10.8	--	--	--	--	--	--	589.3
Maple / beech / birch group	--	--	8.1	--	7.6	--	--	--	--	--	--	--	15.7
Other hardwoods group	--	2.6	9.4	9.0	1.5	--	--	--	--	--	--	--	22.5
Exotic hardwoods group	--	--	22.7	5.2	--	--	--	--	--	--	--	--	27.9
Nonstocked	29.4	--	--	--	--	--	--	--	--	--	--	--	29.4
All forest-type groups	29.4	187.6	962.7	668.8	191.5	64.1	1.3	--	--	--	--	--	2,105.5

All table cells without observations in the inventory sample are indicated by --. Table value of 0.0 indicates the acres round to less than 0.1 thousand acres. Columns and rows may not add to their totals due to rounding.

Table 7.—Area of forest land, in thousand acres, by forest-type group and stand origin, Kansas, 2001-2005

Forest-type group	Stand origin		All forest land
	Natural stands	Artificial regeneration	
White / red / jack pine group	--	3.1	3.1
Other eastern softwoods group	78.4	6.5	85.0
Ponderosa pine group	--	7.1	7.1
Oak / pine group	46.8	4.5	51.3
Oak / hickory group	1,257.7	10.1	1,267.8
Oak / gum / cypress group	6.5	--	6.5
Elm / ash / cottonwood group	586.3	2.9	589.3
Maple / beech / birch group	15.7	--	15.7
Other hardwoods group	22.5	--	22.5
Exotic hardwoods group	22.7	5.2	27.9
Nonstocked	29.4	--	29.4
All forest-type groups	2,066.1	39.4	2,105.5

All table cells without observations in the inventory sample are indicated by --. Table value of 0.0 indicates the acres round to less than 0.1 thousand acres. Columns and rows may not add to their totals due to rounding.

Table 8.— Area of forest land, in thousand acres, by forest-type group and disturbance class, Kansas, 2001-2005

Forest-type group	Disturbance class									All forest land
	None	Insects	Disease	Weather	Fire	Domestic animals	Wild animals	Human	Other	
White / red / jack pine group	3.1	--	--	--	--	--	--	--	--	3.1
Other eastern softwoods group	45.1	--	--	--	1.3	38.6	--	--	--	85.0
Ponderosa pine group	7.1	--	--	--	--	--	--	--	--	7.1
Oak / pine group	20.2	--	--	7.9	2.7	20.5	--	--	--	51.3
Oak / hickory group	651.9	--	--	41.8	110.2	415.7	14.1	34.0	--	1,267.8
Oak / gum / cypress group	1.3	--	--	--	5.2	--	--	--	--	6.5
Elm / ash / cottonwood group	340.4	--	--	66.1	12.0	151.0	5.3	14.5	--	589.3
Maple / beech / birch group	7.6	--	--	--	--	8.1	--	--	--	15.7
Other hardwoods group	22.5	--	--	--	--	--	--	--	--	22.5
Exotic hardwoods group	15.5	--	--	6.0	--	6.4	--	--	--	27.9
Nonstocked	9.2	--	--	1.8	--	17.0	--	1.5	--	29.4
All forest-type groups	**1,123.8**	**--**	**--**	**123.5**	**131.5**	**657.3**	**19.5**	**49.9**	**--**	**2,105.5**

All table cells without observations in the inventory sample are indicated by --. Table value of 0.0 indicates the acres round to less than 0.1 thousand acres. Columns and rows may not add to their totals due to rounding.

Table 9.— Area of timberland, in thousand acres, by forest-type group and stand-size class, Kansas, 2001-2005

Forest-type group	Stand-size class					All size classes
	Large diameter	Medium diameter	Small diameter	Chaparral	Nonstocked	
White / red / jack pine group	3.1	--	--	--	--	3.1
Other eastern softwoods group	10.5	22.5	46.8	--	--	79.8
Ponderosa pine group	--	7.1	--	--	--	7.1
Oak / pine group	17.4	19.8	14.1	--	--	51.3
Oak / hickory group	463.0	552.8	187.1	--	--	1,202.9
Oak / gum / cypress group	--	6.5	--	--	--	6.5
Elm / ash / cottonwood group	449.2	99.6	38.9	--	--	587.7
Maple / beech / birch group	7.6	8.1	--	--	--	15.7
Other hardwoods group	6.0	1.4	10.4	--	--	17.8
Exotic hardwoods group	7.6	12.4	6.4	--	--	26.4
Nonstocked	--	--	--	--	29.4	29.4
All forest-type groups	964.5	730.2	303.6	--	29.4	2,027.7

All table cells without observations in the inventory sample are indicated by --. Table value of 0.0 indicates the acres round to less than 0.1 thousand acres. Columns and rows may not add to their totals due to rounding.

Table 10.—Number of live trees (at least 1 inch d.b.h./d.r.c.), in thousand trees, on forest land by species group and diameter class, Kansas, 2001-2005

Species group	Diameter class (inches)															All classes
	1.0-2.9	3.0-4.9	5.0-6.9	7.0-8.9	9.0-10.9	11.0-12.9	13.0-14.9	15.0-16.9	17.0-18.9	19.0-20.9	21.0-24.9	25.0-28.9	29.0-32.9	33.0-36.9	37.0+	
Softwood species groups																
Eastern softwood species groups																
Loblolly and shortleaf pines	--	--	71	142	71	--	--	--	--	--	--	--	--	--	--	284
Eastern white and red pines	--	--	--	--	35	71	35	71	--	--	--	--	--	--	--	213
Other eastern softwoods	27,147	12,904	7,901	4,658	1,915	1,107	485	228	--	--	--	--	--	--	--	56,346
All softwoods	27,147	12,904	7,972	4,800	2,022	1,178	520	299	--	--	--	--	--	--	--	56,843
Hardwood species groups																
Eastern hardwood species groups																
Select white oaks	13,947	1,949	3,369	2,474	1,965	1,080	589	617	598	438	725	507	197	67	--	28,513
Select red oaks	2,609	1,192	1,167	645	395	410	429	331	283	202	362	168	31	--	--	8,224
Other white oaks	8,942	3,539	5,742	4,484	2,907	980	442	79	--	89	31	--	--	--	--	27,235
Other red oaks	5,488	4,105	1,783	1,686	914	1,293	516	241	221	31	32	31	--	48	--	16,390
Hickory	20,835	3,801	4,231	2,655	1,469	1,040	617	280	104	48	63	31	--	--	--	35,176
Hard maple	9,127	2,076	460	447	194	167	96	--	--	48	--	--	--	--	--	12,614
Soft maple	802	--	333	197	236	100	118	159	113	129	64	35	48	--	--	2,335
Ash	11,773	13,279	6,084	4,469	3,585	2,271	1,578	794	575	240	382	82	--	--	--	45,111
Cottonwood and aspen	457	447	386	615	435	552	496	565	391	357	280	409	72	34	435	5,831
Basswood	1,808	536	181	214	32	75	48	--	--	32	--	--	--	--	--	2,927
Black walnut	6,025	3,439	4,318	3,150	2,500	1,739	1,421	901	429	440	43	--	--	--	--	24,404
Other eastern soft hardwoods	110,147	56,164	31,051	19,576	10,836	6,483	4,007	3,227	1,860	835	864	531	229	67	35	245,913
Other eastern hard hardwoods	22,966	20,000	13,395	8,437	4,964	2,497	1,098	1,032	608	168	337	140	74	--	--	75,707
Eastern noncommercial hardwoods	68,885	30,725	16,561	7,140	4,319	1,651	715	305	344	280	183	85	48	--	--	131,240
All hardwoods	283,810	141,264	89,060	56,089	34,732	20,337	12,121	8,580	5,526	3,340	3,366	2,020	700	216	471	661,621
All species groups	310,957	154,158	97,032	60,889	36,754	21,515	12,641	8,879	5,526	3,340	3,366	2,020	700	216	471	718,464

All table cells without observations in the inventory sample are indicated by --. Table value of 0 indicates the number of trees rounds to less than 1 thousand trees. Columns and rows may not add to their totals due to rounding.

Table 11.— Number of growing-stock trees (at least 5 inches d.b.h.), in thousand trees, on timberland by species group and diameter class, Kansas, 2001-2005

Species group	Diameter class (inches)													All classes
	5.0-6.9	7.0-8.9	9.0-10.9	11.0-12.9	13.0-14.9	15.0-16.9	17.0-18.9	19.0-20.9	21.0-24.9	25.0-28.9	29.0-32.9	33.0-36.9	37.0+	
Softwood species groups														
Eastern softwood species groups														
Loblolly and shortleaf pines	71	106	71	--	--	--	--	--	--	--	--	--	--	248
Eastern white and red pines	--	--	--	35	35	35	--	--	--	--	--	--	--	106
Other eastern softwoods	5,797	3,164	1,136	733	315	144	--	--	--	--	--	--	--	11,289
All softwoods	5,868	3,270	1,207	769	350	179	--	--	--	--	--	--	--	11,644
Hardwood species groups														
Eastern hardwood species groups														
Select white oaks	1,219	1,062	963	744	282	314	266	241	264	314	79	31	--	5,778
Select red oaks	1,071	545	336	311	429	299	251	170	238	132	31	--	--	3,814
Other white oaks	2,785	1,885	1,287	358	205	31	--	31	--	--	--	--	--	6,581
Other red oaks	782	1,038	502	596	310	144	111	31	31	--	--	48	--	3,593
Hickory	3,291	2,172	961	744	497	201	67	--	63	--	--	--	--	7,997
Hard maple	106	350	145	118	96	97	81	--	--	--	--	--	--	815
Soft maple	229	166	145	--	118	--	--	129	31	--	48	--	--	1,044
Ash	4,133	2,591	2,094	1,175	1,118	334	388	175	208	--	--	--	--	12,215
Cottonwood and aspen	321	341	404	482	411	461	320	287	169	296	--	--	333	3,825
Basswood	102	59	32	43	--	--	--	--	--	--	--	--	--	236
Black walnut	2,597	1,709	1,588	697	1,131	623	307	370	--	--	--	--	--	9,023
Other eastern soft hardwoods	15,217	9,172	5,119	2,885	2,100	1,718	867	384	460	296	112	31	35	38,397
Other eastern hard hardwoods	3,903	2,443	1,359	456	166	288	68	136	64	--	--	--	--	8,882
All hardwoods	35,757	23,533	14,996	8,607	6,862	4,509	2,725	1,955	1,497	1,069	270	111	369	102,201
All species groups	41,625	26,804	16,144	9,376	7,212	4,688	2,725	1,955	1,497	1,069	270	111	369	113,845

All table cells without observations in the inventory sample are indicated by --. Table value of 0 indicates the number of trees rounds to less than 1 thousand trees. Columns and rows may not add to their totals due to rounding.

Table 11a.—Number of growing-stock trees, in thousands, on timberland by species and diameter class, Kansas, 2001-2005

Species	Diameter class (inches)										Total
	5-6.9	7-8.9	9-10.9	11-12.9	13-14.9	15-16.9	17-18.9	19-20.9	21-28.9	29.0+	
Softwood species											
Austrian pine	36	0	0	0	0	0	0	0	0	0	36
eastern redcedar	5,761	2,949	1,136	698	272	108	0	0	0	0	10,924
eastern white pine	0	0	0	35	0	0	0	0	0	0	35
ponderosa pine	0	215	0	36	43	36	0	0	0	0	330
red pine	0	0	0	0	35	35	0	0	0	0	71
shortleaf pine	71	106	71	0	0	0	0	0	0	0	248
All softwoods	5,868	3,270	1,207	769	350	179	0	0	0	0	11,644
Hardwood species											
American basswood	102	59	32	43	0	0	0	0	0	0	236
American elm	5,612	3,045	1,385	319	328	230	127	36	43	32	11,156
American sycamore	140	43	107	0	79	166	0	0	274	115	923
bitternut hickory	1,349	668	493	138	226	90	67	0	0	0	3,031
black cherry	155	31	31	32	0	0	0	0	32	0	282
black hickory	0	0	0	47	0	0	0	0	0	0	47
black locust	287	380	151	0	0	0	0	0	0	0	818
black oak	227	264	138	343	279	144	79	0	0	0	1,474
black walnut	2,597	1,709	1,588	697	1,131	623	307	370	0	0	9,023
black willow	177	177	100	171	177	38	70	39	43	0	992
blackjack oak	94	141	47	94	0	0	0	0	0	0	377
blue ash	0	47	0	0	0	0	0	0	0	0	47
boxelder	141	109	211	91	31	0	94	0	0	31	709
bur oak	517	380	454	441	96	196	96	193	354	110	2,836
chinkapin oak	702	683	509	303	186	118	139	48	223	0	2,910
common persimmon	342	110	0	0	0	0	0	0	0	0	452
eastern cottonwood	321	305	368	303	339	205	245	177	319	190	2,772
green ash	2,952	2,258	1,917	986	1,079	334	328	175	170	0	10,198
hackberry	7,558	5,042	2,814	1,897	1,448	1,247	400	309	363	0	21,078
honeylocust	2,448	967	533	283	31	64	32	59	32	0	4,451
Kentucky coffeetree	214	280	190	79	63	117	0	43	0	0	987

(Table 11a continued on next page)

(Table 11a continued)

Species	Diameter class (inches)										Total
	5-6.9	7-8.9	9-10.9	11-12.9	13-14.9	15-16.9	17-18.9	19-20.9	21-28.9	29.0+	
mockernut hickory	32	0	0	0	0	31	0	0	0	0	64
mulberry spp.	150	32	0	59	0	0	0	0	0	0	242
northern catalpa	0	37	110	266	37	37	109	0	0	0	595
northern red oak	1,071	497	305	279	316	268	220	170	370	31	3,527
Ohio buckeye	86	0	0	0	0	0	0	0	0	0	86
overcup oak	0	34	0	0	0	0	0	0	0	0	34
pecan	260	260	161	261	0	47	0	0	63	0	1,052
pin oak	461	633	316	158	31	0	0	31	31	48	1,711
plains cottonwood	0	36	36	179	72	256	74	110	146	143	1,053
post oak	2,785	1,851	1,287	358	205	31	0	31	0	0	6,547
red mulberry	461	637	485	34	71	106	36	34	32	0	1,897
rock elm	0	36	0	0	0	0	0	0	0	0	36
shagbark hickory	1,553	1,115	308	298	222	32	0	0	0	0	3,529
shellbark hickory	97	129	0	0	48	0	0	0	0	0	274
shingle oak	0	0	0	0	0	0	32	0	0	0	32
Shumard oak	0	48	31	31	113	31	31	0	0	0	287
Siberian elm	502	430	251	72	0	0	36	0	0	0	1,291
silver maple	229	166	145	0	118	97	81	129	31	48	1,044
slippery elm	847	258	110	39	0	0	31	0	0	0	1,285
sugar maple	106	350	145	118	96	0	0	0	0	0	815
Texas buckeye	0	0	0	0	0	0	0	0	0	0	0
white ash	1,182	286	177	189	39	0	59	0	39	0	1,970
white oak	0	0	0	0	0	0	31	0	0	0	31
All hardwoods	35,757	23,533	14,936	8,607	6,862	4,509	2,725	1,955	2,566	751	102,201
Total	41,625	26,804	16,144	9,376	7,212	4,688	2,725	1,955	2,566	751	113,845

All table cells without observations in the inventory sample are indicated by --.

42

Table 12.—Net volume of live trees (at least 5 inches d.b.h./d.r.c.), in million cubic feet, by owner class and forest-land status, Kansas, 2001-2005

| Owner class | Unreserved forests | | | Reserved forests | | | All forest land |
	Timberland	Unproductive	Total	Productive	Unproductive	Total	
Other Federal							
Fish and Wildlife Service	4.0	--	4.0	--	--	--	4.0
Department of Defense or Energy	77.8	--	77.8	--	--	--	77.8
Other Federal	18.8	--	18.8	--	--	--	18.8
State and local government							
State	21.1	0.4	21.5	--	--	--	21.5
Local (county, municipal, etc.)	37.8	--	37.8	1.6	--	1.6	39.4
Private							
Undifferentiated private	2,517.4	62.6	2,580.1	--	--	--	2,580.1
All owners	2,676.9	63.0	2,739.9	1.6	--	1.6	2,741.5

All table cells without observations in the inventory sample are indicated by --. Table value of 0.0 indicates the volume rounds to less than 0.1 million cubic feet. Columns and rows may not add to their totals due to rounding.

Table 13. — Net volume of live trees (at least 5 inches d.b.h./d.r.c.), in million cubic feet, on forest land by forest-type group and stand-size class, Kansas, 2001-2005

Forest-type group	Stand-size class					All size classes
	Large diameter	Medium diameter	Small diameter	Chaparral	Nonstocked	
White / red / jack pine group	6.2	--	--	--	--	6.2
Other eastern softwoods group	13.0	15.6	7.5	--	--	36.2
Ponderosa pine group	--	4.4	--	--	--	4.4
Oak / pine group	28.1	9.2	1.8	--	--	39.1
Oak / hickory group	825.8	470.1	30.9	--	--	1,326.7
Oak / gum / cypress group	--	9.3	--	--	--	9.3
Elm / ash / cottonwood group	1,132.7	97.0	10.8	--	--	1,240.6
Maple / beech / birch group	4.9	9.4	--	--	--	14.4
Other hardwoods group	16.3	4.4	1.6	--	--	22.3
Exotic hardwoods group	24.4	14.0	0.2	--	--	38.6
Nonstocked	--	--	--	--	3.7	3.7
All forest-type groups	2,051.6	633.5	52.7	--	3.7	2,741.5

All table cells without observations in the inventory sample are indicated by --. Table value of 0.0 indicates the volume rounds to less than 0.1 million cubic feet. Columns and rows may not add to their totals due to rounding.

Table 13a.–Net volume of all live trees, in million cubic feet, on forest land by species and forest type group, Kansas, 2001-2005

Species	White / red / jack pine	Other eastern softwoods	Ponderosa pine	Oak / pine	Oak / hickory	Oak / gum / cypress	Elm / ash / cottonwood	Maple / beech / birch	Other hardwoods	Exotic hardwoods	Nonstocked	All forest type groups
ailanthus	-	-	-	-	-	-	0.3	-	-	-	-	0.3
American basswood	-	-	-	-	4.8	-	0.6	-	-	-	-	5.4
American elm	-	1.4	0.1	3.3	106.7	2.2	100.2	0.6	0.4	-	-	214.9
American hornbeam, musclewood	-	-	-	-	0.2	-	-	-	-	-	-	0.2
American plum	-	-	-	-	-	-	0.3	-	-	-	-	0.3
American sycamore	-	-	-	-	30.8	-	59.5	-	-	-	-	90.3
apple spp.	-	-	-	-	-	-	-	-	-	-	-	-
Austrian pine	-	-	-	-	0.1	-	-	-	-	-	-	0.1
bitternut hickory	-	-	-	0.1	28.7	-	3.0	-	-	-	-	31.8
black cherry	-	-	-	-	8.3	-	0.5	-	-	-	-	8.7
black hickory	-	-	-	-	2.7	-	-	-	-	-	-	2.7
black locust	-	-	-	0.4	6.6	-	-	-	0.8	-	-	7.8
black oak	-	-	-	-	26.9	-	-	-	-	-	-	26.9
black walnut	-	0.3	0.1	4.8	102.9	1.0	55.7	-	-	-	-	164.7
black willow	-	-	-	0.9	3.6	-	25.4	-	-	3.0	3.0	35.8
blackjack oak	-	-	-	-	16.4	-	-	-	-	-	-	16.4
blue ash	-	-	-	-	0.2	-	-	-	-	-	-	0.2
boxelder	-	-	-	-	2.5	-	35.6	-	-	-	-	38.1
bur oak	-	-	-	-	130.0	-	24.3	-	-	-	-	154.3
cherry and plum spp.	-	-	-	-	0.1	-	-	-	-	-	-	0.1
chinkapin oak	-	-	0.1	0.5	89.8	-	1.8	3.3	0.1	-	-	95.4
chittamwood, gum bumelia	-	-	-	-	0.3	0.1	-	-	-	-	-	0.4
chokecherry	-	-	-	-	-	-	-	-	-	-	-	-
common persimmon	-	-	-	0.2	1.4	-	0.0	-	-	-	-	1.6
downy hawthorn	-	-	-	-	-	-	-	-	-	-	-	-
eastern cottonwood	-	-	-	-	12.8	-	225.5	-	-	1.5	-	239.8
eastern hophornbeam	-	-	-	-	0.7	-	-	-	-	-	-	0.7
eastern redbud	-	-	-	-	4.8	-	1.4	0.1	-	-	-	6.4
eastern redcedar	-	28.7	0.6	16.8	20.2	-	6.0	0.3	-	0.1	-	72.8
eastern white pine	1.6	-	-	-	-	-	-	-	-	-	-	1.6
green ash	-	0.2	-	5.0	79.5	0.4	126.0	-	0.7	0.5	-	212.3
hackberry	-	0.3	-	2.8	82.3	0.8	260.1	-	4.9	0.6	0.3	352.1
hawthorn spp.	-	-	-	-	-	-	-	-	-	-	-	-
honeylocust	-	0.3	-	0.4	83.2	-	8.7	-	0.3	-	-	92.8
Kentucky coffeetree	-	-	-	-	8.9	-	7.6	-	-	-	-	16.4
mockernut hickory	-	-	-	-	0.3	-	1.4	-	-	-	-	1.7
mulberry spp.	-	-	-	-	0.4	-	3.7	-	-	-	-	4.1
northern catalpa	-	0.5	-	-	5.1	-	-	-	14.0	-	-	19.6
northern red oak	-	-	-	-	93.0	-	2.8	2.5	-	-	-	98.2
Ohio buckeye	-	-	-	-	-	-	0.3	-	-	-	-	0.3
Osage-orange	-	1.3	0.2	0.2	139.9	-	29.6	-	0.3	-	0.2	171.6
overcup oak	-	-	-	-	-	-	0.1	-	-	-	-	0.1

(Table 13a continued on next page)

(Table 13a continued)

Species	White / red / jack pine	Other eastern softwoods	Ponderosa pine	Oak / pine	Oak / hickory	Oak / gum / cypress	Elm / ash / cottonwood	Maple / beech / birch	Other hardwoods	Exotic hardwoods	Nonstocked groups	All forest type
pawpaw	-	-	-	-	-	-	-	-	-	-	-	-
peachleaf willow	-	-	-	1.2	2.4	-	3.4	-	-	-	-	7.0
pecan	-	0.3	-	-	3.2	-	23.0	-	-	-	-	26.5
pin oak	-	-	-	-	20.4	1.6	6.4	-	-	-	-	28.4
plains cottonwood	-	-	-	-	-	-	113.6	-	-	-	-	113.6
ponderosa pine	-	2.7	3.5	-	-	-	-	-	-	-	-	6.2
post oak	-	-	-	-	76.6	-	-	-	-	-	-	76.6
red maple	-	-	-	0.0	-	-	-	-	-	-	-	0.0
red mulberry	-	-	-	2.5	62.7	-	53.0	-	0.2	0.0	0.0	118.5
red pine	2.9	-	-	-	-	-	-	-	-	-	-	2.9
rock elm	-	-	-	-	-	-	-	-	-	-	-	0.2
Russian-olive	-	-	-	-	0.2	-	0.2	-	-	-	-	0.2
serviceberry spp.	-	-	-	-	-	-	-	-	-	-	-	0.2
shagbark hickory	-	-	-	-	24.9	-	1.5	-	-	-	-	26.4
shellbark hickory	-	-	-	-	0.9	-	1.5	-	-	-	-	2.3
shingle oak	-	-	-	-	3.8	-	-	-	-	-	-	3.8
shortleaf pine	1.7	-	-	-	-	-	-	-	-	-	-	1.7
Shumard oak	-	-	-	-	2.6	3.1	-	-	-	-	-	5.7
Siberian elm	-	0.2	-	-	2.5	-	0.5	-	-	32.8	-	36.0
silver maple	-	-	-	-	0.5	-	42.3	-	-	-	-	42.8
slippery elm	-	0.1	-	0.1	8.3	-	4.6	-	-	-	-	13.1
southern catalpa	-	-	-	-	-	-	1.3	-	-	-	-	1.3
sugar maple	-	-	-	-	6.0	-	-	5.9	-	-	-	11.9
sugarberry	-	-	-	-	0.7	-	1.7	-	-	-	-	2.4
Texas buckeye	-	-	-	-	-	-	0.9	-	-	-	-	0.9
western soapberry	-	-	-	-	-	-	0.5	-	0.7	-	-	1.2
white ash	-	-	-	-	9.9	-	5.6	1.7	-	-	-	17.2
white mulberry	-	-	-	-	0.3	-	0.7	-	-	-	-	1.0
white oak	-	-	-	-	6.9	-	0.1	-	-	-	-	6.9
white willow	-	-	-	-	-	-	-	-	-	-	-	0.1
All species	6.2	36.2	4.4	39.1	1,326.7	9.3	1,240.6	14.4	22.3	38.6	3.7	2,741.5

46

Table 14.—Net volume of live trees (at least 5 inches d.b.h./d.r.c.), in million cubic feet, on forest land by species group and ownership group, Kansas, 2001-2005

Species group	Ownership group				
	Forest Service	Other Federal	State and local government	Undifferentiated private	All owners
Softwood species groups					
Eastern softwood species groups					
Loblolly and shortleaf pines	--	1.7	--	--	1.7
Eastern white and red pines	--	4.5	--	--	4.5
Other eastern softwoods	--	5.7	0.8	72.5	79.0
All softwoods	--	11.9	0.8	72.5	85.3
Hardwood species groups					
Eastern hardwood species groups					
Select white oaks	--	5.6	4.4	246.7	256.6
Select red oaks	--	2.6	2.4	98.9	103.9
Other white oaks	--	--	5.0	71.7	76.7
Other red oaks	--	0.2	4.0	71.2	75.4
Hickory	--	0.4	2.2	88.8	91.4
Hard maple	--	--	1.1	10.8	11.9
Soft maple	--	8.9	1.5	32.5	42.9
Ash	--	11.3	0.6	217.7	229.6
Cottonwood and aspen	--	31.4	23.9	298.0	353.4
Basswood	--	--	--	5.4	5.4
Black walnut	--	2.8	0.2	161.6	164.7
Other eastern soft hardwoods	--	14.3	7.2	790.8	812.3
Other eastern hard hardwoods	--	7.1	5.6	229.7	242.4
Eastern noncommercial hardwoods	--	4.1	1.9	183.6	189.5
All hardwoods	--	88.7	60.1	2,507.5	2,656.3
All species groups	--	100.6	60.9	2,580.1	2,741.5

All table cells without observations in the inventory sample are indicated by --. Table value of 0.0 indicates the volume rounds to less than 0.1 million cubic feet. Columns and rows may not add to their totals due to rounding.

Table 15. — Net volume of live trees (at least 5 inches d.b.h./d.r.c.), in million cubic feet, on forest land by species group and diameter class, Kansas, 2001-2005

Species group	5.0-6.9	7.0-8.9	9.0-10.9	11.0-12.9	13.0-14.9	15.0-16.9	17.0-18.9	19.0-20.9	21.0-24.9	25.0-28.9	29.0-32.9	33.0-36.9	37.0+	All classes
Softwood species groups														
Eastern softwood species groups														
Loblolly and shortleaf pines	0	1	1	--	--	--	--	--	--	--	--	--	--	2
Eastern white and red pines	--	--	0	1	1	2	--	--	--	--	--	--	--	5
Other eastern softwoods	16	20	15	14	9	6	--	--	--	--	--	--	--	79
All softwoods	16	21	16	15	9	8	--	--	--	--	--	--	--	85
Hardwood species groups														
Eastern hardwood species groups														
Select white oaks	7	11	17	16	12	17	24	21	47	49	25	11	--	257
Select red oaks	3	3	4	6	9	11	11	10	24	18	5	--	--	104
Other white oaks	11	18	21	11	7	2	--	4	2	--	--	--	--	77
Other red oaks	3	8	7	15	10	7	8	1	3	4	9	--	--	75
Hickory	10	13	13	16	15	10	5	3	5	3	--	--	--	91
Hard maple	1	2	2	3	2	--	--	2	--	--	--	--	--	12
Soft maple	1	1	2	1	3	5	5	8	5	4	8	--	--	43
Ash	13	21	31	33	34	24	24	14	29	8	--	--	--	230
Cottonwood and aspen	1	3	5	9	12	19	18	21	22	52	12	6	174	353
Basswood	0	1	0	1	--	1	--	1	--	--	--	--	--	5
Black walnut	9	15	21	23	29	26	16	22	3	--	--	--	--	165
Other eastern soft hardwoods	62	86	89	86	83	98	72	43	64	62	35	15	18	812
Other eastern hard hardwoods	24	34	36	30	20	26	21	9	21	13	8	--	--	242
Eastern noncommercial hardwoods	29	29	34	22	13	8	13	14	11	9	7	--	--	190
All hardwoods	174	244	283	271	249	254	218	173	238	221	100	41	192	2,656
All species groups	189	265	298	286	258	262	218	173	238	221	100	41	192	2,742

All table cells without observations in the inventory sample are indicated by --. Table value of 0 indicates the volume rounds to less than 1 million cubic feet. Columns and rows may not add to their totals due to rounding.

Table 15a.—Net volume of all live trees, in million cubic feet, on forest land by species and diameter class, Kansas, 2001-2005

Species	Diameter class (inches)										Total
	5.0-6.9	7.0-8.9	9.0-10.9	11.0-12.9	13.0-14.9	15.0-16.9	17.0-18.9	19.0-20.9	21.0-28.9	29.0+	
Softwood species											
Austrian pine	0	0	0	0	0	0	0	0	0	0	0
eastern redcedar	16	19	15	13	6	4	0	0	0	0	73
eastern white pine	0	0	0	1	0	1	0	0	0	0	2
ponderosa pine	0	1	0	1	2	2	0	0	0	0	6
red pine	0	0	0	1	1	1	0	0	0	0	3
shortleaf pine	0	1	1	0	0	0	0	0	0	0	2
All softwoods	16	21	16	15	9	8	0	0	0	0	85
Hardwood species											
ailanthus	0	0	0	0	0	0	0	0	0	0	0
American basswood	0	1	0	1	0	1	0	1	0	0	5
American elm	26	36	33	24	25	25	17	9	15	4	215
American hornbeam, musclewood	0	0		0	0	0	0	0	0	0	0
American plum	0	0	0	0	0	0	0	0	0	0	0
American sycamore	0	0	1	0	3	7	0	0	43	36	90
bitternut hickory	4	4	6	5	6	3	3	0	0	0	32
black cherry	1	1	2	0	0	0	0	2	2	0	9
black hickory	0	0	0	1	0	2	0	0	0	0	3
black locust	0	4	2	2	6	0	0	2	0	0	8
black oak	0	1	2	7	6	4	5	0	0	0	27
black walnut	9	15	21	23	29	26	16	22	3	0	165
black willow	1	2	2	5	6	2	10	2	5	0	36
blackjack oak	2	3	2	6	2	2	0	0	0	0	16
blue ash	0	0	0	0	0	0	0	0	0	0	0
boxelder	2	4	6	8	3	3	5	2	3	4	38
bur oak	3	3	7	9	5	11	13	13	68	21	154
cherry and plum spp.	0	0	0	0	0	0	0	0	0	0	0
chinkapin oak	4	8	10	6	7	6	10	7	28	9	95
chittamwood, gum bumelia	0	0	0	0	0	0	0	0	0	0	0
common persimmon	1	0	0	0	0	0	0	0	0	0	2
eastern cottonwood	1	2	4	6	10	10	13	12	56	124	240
eastern hophornbeam	0	0	0	0	0	0	0	0	0	0	1
eastern redbud	4	2	1	0	0	0	0	0	0	0	6
green ash	10	19	30	30	33	22	22	14	34	0	212
hackberry	24	33	36	39	44	59	26	26	48	18	352
honeylocust	9	12	13	12	6	10	8	5	13	5	93
Kentucky coffeetree	1	2	2	2	2	4	0	3	0	0	16
mockernut hickory	0	0	1	0	0	1	0	0	0	0	2

(Table 15a continued on next page)

(Table 15a continued)

Species	Diameter class (inches)										Total
	5.0-6.9	7.0-8.9	9.0-10.9	11.0-12.9	13.0-14.9	15.0-16.9	17.0-18.9	19.0-20.9	21.0-28.9	29.0+	
mulberry spp.	1	1	0	1	1	0	0	0	0	0	4
northern catalpa	1	1	1	5	2	1	5	0	4	0	20
northern red oak	3	3	3	5	7	10	10	10	42	5	98
Ohio buckeye	0	0	0	0	0	0	0	0	0	0	0
Osage-orange	24	26	32	21	13	8	8	13	21	7	172
overcup oak	0	0	0	0	0	0	0	0	0	0	0
peachleaf willow	0	0	0	0	0	0	5	1	0	0	7
pecan	1	2	2	5	2	2	2	3	8	0	26
pin oak	1	4	3	2	2	0	2	1	4	9	28
plains cottonwood	0	0	0	3	2	9	5	8	18	68	114
post oak	11	18	21	11	7	2	0	4	2	0	77
red maple	0	0	0	0	0	0	0	0	0	0	0
red mulberry	10	15	18	14	11	12	14	2	21	3	118
rock elm	0	0	0	0	0	0	0	0	0	0	0
Russian-olive	0	0	0	0	0	0	0	0	0	0	0
shagbark hickory	4	6	4	6	5	2	0	0	0	0	26
shellbark hickory	0	1	0	0	1	0	0	0	0	0	2
shingle oak	0	0	0	0	0	0	1	0	3	0	4
Shumard oak	0	0	0	1	2	1	1	0	0	0	6
Siberian elm	2	5	5	4	0	3	5	2	7	5	36
silver maple	1	1	2	1	3	5	5	8	9	8	43
slippery elm	3	3	3	1	1	0	2	0	0	0	13
southern catalpa	0	0	1	0	0	0	0	0	0	0	1
sugar maple	1	2	2	3	2	0	0	2	0	0	12
sugarberry	0	0	1	0	0	0	2	0	0	0	2
Texas buckeye	1	0	0	0	0	0	0	0	0	0	1
western soapberry	0	0	0	0	0	0	0	0	0	0	1
white ash	2	2	2	3	1	2	2	0	3	0	17
white mulberry	0	0	0	1	0	0	0	0	0	0	1
white oak	0	0	0	0	0	0	1	0	0	6	7
white willow	0	0	0	0	0	0	0	0	0	0	0
All hardwoods	174	244	283	271	249	254	218	173	459	333	2,656
All species	189	265	298	286	258	262	218	173	459	333	2,742

All table cells without observations in the inventory sample are indicated by --.
Table value of 0 indicates the volume rounds to less than 1 million cubic feet.
Columns and rows may not add to their totals due to rounding.

Table 16.—Net volume of live trees (at least 5 inches d.b.h./d.r.c.), in million cubic feet, on forest land by forest-type group and stand origin, Kansas, 2001-2005

| Forest-type group | Stand origin | | All forest land |
	Natural stands	Artificial regeneration	
White / red / jack pine group	--	6.2	6.2
Other eastern softwoods group	28.1	8.1	36.2
Ponderosa pine group	--	4.4	4.4
Oak / pine group	32.6	6.5	39.1
Oak / hickory group	1,318.7	8.1	1,326.7
Oak / gum / cypress group	9.3	--	9.3
Elm / ash / cottonwood group	1,237.8	2.8	1,240.6
Maple / beech / birch group	14.4	--	14.4
Other hardwoods group	22.3	--	22.3
Exotic hardwoods group	25.6	13.0	38.6
Nonstocked	3.7	--	3.7
All forest-type groups	**2,692.5**	**49.1**	**2,741.5**

All table cells without observations in the inventory sample are indicated by --. Table value of 0.0 indicates the volume rounds to less than 0.1 million cubic feet. Columns and rows may not add to their totals due to rounding.

Table 17.— Net volume of growing-stock trees (at least 5 inches d.b.h.), in million cubic feet, on timberland by species group and diameter class, Kansas, 2001-2005

Species group	Diameter class (inches)													All classes
	5.0-6.9	7.0-8.9	9.0-10.9	11.0-12.9	13.0-14.9	15.0-16.9	17.0-18.9	19.0-20.9	21.0-24.9	25.0-28.9	29.0-32.9	33.0-36.9	37.0+	
Softwood species groups														
Eastern softwood species groups														
Loblolly and shortleaf pines	0	1	1	--	--	--	--	--	--	--	--	--	--	2
Eastern white and red pines	--	--	--	1	1	1	--	--	--	--	--	--	--	2
Other eastern softwoods	12	14	9	9	6	4	--	--	--	--	--	--	--	53
All softwoods	12	14	9	10	6	5	--	--	--	--	--	--	--	57
Hardwood species groups														
Eastern hardwood species groups														
Select white oaks	3	5	8	11	6	9	11	11	18	30	11	5	--	129
Select red oaks	3	3	3	5	9	10	10	9	17	14	5	--	--	88
Other white oaks	6	8	10	4	4	1	1	1	--	--	--	--	--	34
Other red oaks	2	5	4	8	6	4	5	1	5	4	--	9	--	49
Hickory	8	11	9	12	12	7	3	--	5	--	--	--	--	67
Hard maple	0	2	2	2	2	--	--	--	--	--	--	--	--	8
Soft maple	1	1	1	--	3	3	4	8	2	--	8	--	--	32
Ash	9	13	19	18	25	11	17	10	16	--	--	--	--	138
Cottonwood and aspen	1	2	4	8	10	16	15	17	14	38	--	--	127	251
Basswood	0	0	0	1	--	--	--	--	--	--	--	--	--	2
Black walnut	5	8	13	9	24	18	12	19	--	--	--	--	--	110
Other eastern soft hardwoods	31	42	43	40	45	54	35	21	37	38	19	8	18	430
Other eastern hard hardwoods	8	11	11	6	4	9	3	8	4	--	--	--	--	63
All hardwoods	76	110	129	124	150	143	114	106	114	124	43	22	145	1,400
All species groups	87	124	139	133	157	148	114	106	114	124	43	22	145	1,457

All table cells without observations in the inventory sample are indicated by --. Table value of 0 indicates the volume rounds to less than 1 million cubic feet. Columns and rows may not add to their totals due to rounding.

Table 17a.—Net volume of growing-stock trees, in million cubic feet, on timberland by species and diameter class, Kansas, 2001-2005

Species	Diameter class (inches)										Total
	5.0-6.9	7.0-8.9	9.0-10.9	11.0-12.9	13.0-14.9	15.0-16.9	17.0-18.9	19.0-20.9	21.0-28.9	29.0+	
Softwood species											
Austrian pine	0	0	0	0	0	0	0	0	0	0	0
eastern redcedar	12	13	9	9	5	3	0	0	0	0	49
eastern white pine	0	0	0	1	0	0	0	0	0	0	1
ponderosa pine	0	1	0	1	1	1	0	0	0	0	4
red pine	0	0	0	0	1	1	0	0	0	0	2
shortleaf pine	0	1	1	0	0	0	0	0	0	0	2
All softwoods	12	14	9	10	6	5	0	0	0	0	57
Hardwood species											
American basswood	0	0	0	1	0	0	0	0	0	0	2
American elm	11	13	12	4	7	7	5	2	3	4	69
American sycamore	0	0	1	0	2	7	0	0	34	36	81
bitternut hickory	3	3	5	2	6	3	3	0	0	0	26
black cherry	0	0	0	0	0	0	0	0	2	0	4
black hickory	0	0	0	1	0	0	0	0	0	0	1
black locust	1	1	1	0	0	0	0	0	0	0	3
black oak	0	1	1	5	6	4	3	0	0	0	21
black walnut	5	8	13	9	24	18	12	19	0	0	110
black willow	0	1	1	3	4	1	3	2	5	0	19
blackjack oak	0	1	0	1	0	0	0	0	0	0	2
blue ash	0	0	0	0	0	0	0	0	0	0	0
boxelder	0	0	2	1	1	0	4	0	0	4	13
bur oak	1	2	4	6	2	6	4	9	29	16	79
chinkapin oak	1	3	5	4	4	3	6	2	19	0	49
common persimmon	1	0	0	0	0	0	0	0	0	0	1
eastern cottonwood	1	2	4	5	8	7	12	11	38	77	164
green ash	7	11	17	15	24	11	14	10	13	0	124
hackberry	15	23	23	27	31	38	16	17	30	0	220
honeylocust	5	4	4	4	1	2	1	3	2	0	25
Kentucky coffeetree	0	1	2	1	2	4	0	3	0	0	12
mockernut hickory	0	0	0	0	0	1	0	0	0	0	1
mulberry spp.	0	0	0	1	0	0	0	0	0	0	1
northern catalpa	0	0	1	4	1	1	4	0	0	0	11
northern red oak	3	3	3	4	7	9	9	9	32	5	83

(Table 17a continued on next page)

53

(Table 17a continued)

Species	Diameter class (inches)										
	5.0-6.9	7.0-8.9	9.0-10.9	11.0-12.9	13.0-14.9	15.0-16.9	17.0-18.9	19.0-20.9	21.0-28.9	29.0+	Total
Ohio buckeye	0	0	0	0	0	0	0	0	0	0	0
overcup oak	0	0	0	0	0	0	0	0	0	0	0
pecan	1	1	1	0	0	2	0	0	5	0	14
pin oak	1	3	3	4	1	0	0	1	4	9	24
plains cottonwood	0	0	0	3	2	9	3	6	14	50	88
post oak	6	8	10	4	4	1	0	1	0	0	33
red mulberry	1	3	4	1	2	3	1	2	2	0	20
rock elm	0	0	0	0	0	0	0	0	0	0	0
shagbark hickory	4	6	3	5	5	1	0	0	0	0	23
shellbark hickory	0	1	0	0	1	0	0	0	0	0	2
shingle oak	0	0	0	0	0	0	1	0	0	0	1
Shumard oak	0	0	0	1	2	1	1	0	0	0	6
Siberian elm	1	2	2	1	0	0	2	0	0	0	7
silver maple	1	1	1	0	3	3	4	8	2	8	32
slippery elm	2	1	1	1	0	0	1	0	0	0	6
sugar maple	0	2	2	2	2	0	0	0	0	0	8
white ash	2	1	1	3	1	0	2	0	3	0	14
white oak	0	0	0	0	0	0	1	0	0	0	1
All hardwoods	76	110	129	124	150	143	114	106	238	210	1,400
All species	87	124	139	133	157	148	114	106	238	210	1,457

All table cells without observations in the inventory sample are indicated by --.

Table value of 0 indicates the volume rounds to less than 1 million cubi

Columns and rows may not add to their totals due to rounding.

Table 18.—Net volume of growing-stock trees (at least 5 inches d.b.h.), in million cubic feet, on timberland by species group and ownership group, Kansas, 2001-2005

| Species group | Ownership group | | | | |
	Forest Service	Other Federal	State and local government	Undifferentiated private	All owners
Softwood species groups					
Eastern softwood species groups					
Loblolly and shortleaf pines	--	1.5	--	--	1.5
Eastern white and red pines	--	2.5	--	--	2.5
Other eastern softwoods	--	4.1	0.1	48.7	52.9
All softwoods	--	8.1	0.1	48.7	56.9
Hardwood species groups					
Eastern hardwood species groups					
Select white oaks	--	3.4	3.4	122.6	129.4
Select red oaks	--	2.6	2.2	83.6	88.4
Other white oaks	--	--	2.8	30.8	33.6
Other red oaks	--	0.2	1.5	47.1	48.7
Hickory	--	0.4	2.2	64.3	66.9
Hard maple	--	--	1.1	6.8	7.9
Soft maple	--	8.4	0.8	22.5	31.7
Ash	--	7.3	0.6	129.8	137.7
Cottonwood and aspen	--	31.4	22.4	197.4	251.2
Basswood	--	--	--	1.5	1.5
Black walnut	--	2.0	--	107.8	109.8
Other eastern soft hardwoods	--	6.5	4.3	419.3	430.1
Other eastern hard hardwoods	--	1.7	0.9	60.3	62.9
All hardwoods	--	64.0	42.3	1,293.7	1,400.0
All species groups	--	72.1	42.4	1,342.4	1,456.9

All table cells without observations in the inventory sample are indicated by --. Table value of 0.0 indicates the volume rounds to less than 0.1 million cubic feet. Columns and rows may not add to their totals due to rounding.

Table 19. — Net volume of sawtimber trees (International 1/4-inch rule), in million board feet, on timberland by species group and diameter class, Kansas, 2001-2005

Species group	Diameter class (inches)											All classes
	9.0-10.9	11.0-12.9	13.0-14.9	15.0-16.9	17.0-18.9	19.0-20.9	21.0-24.9	25.0-28.9	29.0-32.9	33.0-36.9	37.0+	
Softwood species groups												
Eastern softwood species groups												
Loblolly and shortleaf pines	3	--	--	--	--	--	--	--	--	--	--	3
Eastern white and red pines	--	2	3	6	--	--	--	--	--	--	--	11
Other eastern softwoods	47	46	28	20	--	--	--	--	--	--	--	140
All softwoods	50	48	31	25	--	--	--	--	--	--	--	154
Hardwood species groups												
Eastern hardwood species groups												
Select white oaks	--	52	29	45	57	56	91	156	57	28	--	572
Select red oaks	--	22	45	48	51	47	90	75	27	--	--	405
Other white oaks	--	19	18	5	--	6	--	--	--	--	--	48
Other red oaks	--	37	30	22	23	7	--	19	--	48	--	185
Hickory	--	56	60	35	17	--	24	--	--	--	--	193
Hard maple	--	10	11	--	--	--	--	--	--	--	--	21
Soft maple	--	--	12	15	18	37	11	--	42	--	--	135
Ash	--	74	109	52	78	50	81	--	--	--	--	444
Cottonwood and aspen	--	35	46	73	74	85	72	203	--	--	583	1,169
Basswood	--	3	--	--	--	--	--	--	--	--	--	3
Black walnut	--	41	110	87	59	92	--	--	--	--	--	388
Other eastern soft hardwoods	--	179	201	250	157	99	181	191	97	44	94	1,493
Other eastern hard hardwoods	--	25	17	39	12	34	20	--	--	--	--	146
All hardwoods	--	553	688	670	544	513	570	644	224	120	676	5,202
All species groups	50	601	719	696	544	513	570	644	224	120	676	5,356

All table cells without observations in the inventory sample are indicated by --. Table value of 0 indicates the volume rounds to less than 1 million board feet. Columns and rows may not add to their totals due to rounding.

Table 19a.—Net volume of sawtimber trees (Doyle rule), in million board feet, on timberland by species group and diameter class, Kansas, 2001-2005

| Species group | Diameter class (inches) | | | | | | | | | | | | All classes |
	9.0-10.9	11.0-12.9	13.0-14.9	15.0-16.9	17.0-18.9	19.0-20.9	21.0-24.9	25.0-28.9	29.0-32.9	33.0-36.9	37.0+	
Softwood species groups												
Eastern softwood species groups												
Loblolly and shortleaf pines	1	--	--	--	--	--	--	--	--	--	--	1
Eastern white and red pines	--	1	2	4	--	--	--	--	--	--	--	7
Other eastern softwoods	16	22	17	14	--	--	--	--	--	--	--	68
All softwoods	17	23	18	18	--	--	--	--	--	--	--	76
Hardwood species groups												
Eastern hardwood species groups												
Select white oaks	--	22	15	27	37	40	72	138	65	32	--	448
Select red oaks	--	9	23	28	33	34	71	67	31	--	--	296
Other white oaks	--	8	9	3	--	5	--	--	--	--	--	24
Other red oaks	--	15	15	13	15	5	--	18	--	54	--	136
Hickory	--	23	31	21	11	--	20	--	--	--	--	106
Hard maple	--	4	6	--	--	--	--	--	--	--	--	10
Soft maple	--	--	6	9	12	26	9	--	48	--	--	110
Ash	--	31	56	30	51	36	67	--	--	--	--	271
Cottonwood and aspen	--	15	23	43	49	61	58	185	--	--	661	1,094
Basswood	--	1	--	--	--	--	--	--	--	--	--	1
Black walnut	--	17	56	51	38	66	--	--	--	--	--	229
Other eastern soft hardwoods	--	75	103	147	103	71	145	176	110	50	106	1,086
Other eastern hard hardwoods	--	10	9	23	8	25	15	--	--	--	--	89
All hardwoods	--	231	352	394	358	368	456	583	254	136	768	3,899
All species groups	17	253	371	412	358	368	456	583	254	136	768	3,976

All table cells without observations in the inventory sample are indicated by --. Table value of 0 indicates the volume rounds to less than 1 million board feet. Columns and rows may not add to their totals due to rounding.

Table 20.—Net volume of saw-log portion of sawtimber trees, in million cubic feet, on timberland by species group and ownership group, Kansas, 2001-2005

Species group	Ownership group				All owners
	Forest Service	Other Federal	State and local government	Undifferentiated private	
Softwood species groups					
Eastern softwood species groups					
Loblolly and shortleaf pines	--	0.6	--	--	0.6
Eastern white and red pines	--	2.3	--	--	2.3
Other eastern softwoods	--	2.1	--	22.0	24.0
All softwoods	--	4.9	--	22.0	26.9
Hardwood species groups					
Eastern hardwood species groups					
Select white oaks	--	1.9	2.3	99.3	103.5
Select red oaks	--	2.4	2.0	68.5	72.9
Other white oaks	--	--	--	7.6	7.6
Other red oaks	--	--	1.1	31.8	32.9
Hickory	--	0.3	0.4	31.5	32.2
Hard maple	--	--	0.8	2.6	3.3
Soft maple	--	7.8	--	18.8	26.7
Ash	--	3.7	0.5	78.9	83.1
Cottonwood and aspen	--	27.5	20.7	185.7	233.9
Basswood	--	--	--	0.5	0.5
Black walnut	--	1.2	--	68.0	69.1
Other eastern soft hardwoods	--	4.1	2.8	269.2	276.1
Other eastern hard hardwoods	--	0.7	0.5	26.8	28.0
All hardwoods	--	49.6	31.1	889.0	969.8
All species groups	--	54.5	31.1	911.0	996.7

All table cells without observations in the inventory sample are indicated by --. Table value of 0.0 indicates the volume rounds to less than 0.1 million cubic feet. Columns and rows may not add to their totals due to rounding.

Table 31.—Aboveground dry weight of live trees (at least 1 inch d.b.h./d.r.c.), in thousand dry short tons, by owner class and forest-land status, Kansas, 2001-2005

Owner class	Unreserved forests			Reserved forests			All forest land
	Timberland	Unproductive	Total	Productive	Unproductive	Total	
Other Federal							
Fish and Wildlife Service	77	--	77	--	--	--	77
Department of Defense or Energy	1,842	--	1,842	--	--	--	1,842
Other Federal	492	--	492	--	--	--	492
State and local government							
State	604	8	613	--	--	--	613
Local (county, municipal, etc.)	825	--	825	39	--	39	863
Private							
Undifferentiated private	66,980	2,134	69,114	--	--	--	69,114
All owners	70,819	2,143	72,962	39	--	39	73,001

All table cells without observations in the inventory sample are indicated by --. Table value of 0 indicates the aboveground tree biomass rounds to less than 1 thousand dry tons. Columns and rows may not add to their totals due to rounding.

Table 32. – Aboveground dry weight of live trees (at least 1 inch d.b.h./d.r.c.), in thousand dry short tons, on forest land by species group and diameter class, Kansas, 2001-2005

Species group	|| Diameter class (inches)															All classes
	1.0-2.9	3.0-4.9	5.0-6.9	7.0-8.9	9.0-10.9	11.0-12.9	13.0-14.9	15.0-16.9	17.0-18.9	19.0-20.9	21.0-22.9	23.0-24.9	25.0-26.9	27.0-28.9	29.0+	
Softwood species groups																
Eastern softwood species groups																
Loblolly and shortleaf pines	--	--	3	18	14	--	--	--	--	--	--	--	--	--	--	35
Eastern white and red pines	--	--	--	--	4	20	13	39	--	--	--	--	--	--	--	76
Other eastern softwoods	79	193	310	387	282	261	161	112	--	--	--	--	--	--	--	1,784
All softwoods	79	193	313	405	300	280	174	151	--	--	--	--	--	--	--	1,895
Hardwood species groups																
Eastern hardwood species groups																
Select white oaks	76	57	234	358	505	441	343	476	656	562	689	574	964	308	925	7,168
Select red oaks	12	40	101	105	110	172	266	298	315	289	585	75	374	113	136	2,990
Other white oaks	52	104	386	575	656	325	220	62	--	111	--	65	--	--	--	2,556
Other red oaks	28	157	120	243	218	460	289	191	234	42	--	72	--	100	246	2,401
Hickory	92	137	344	424	417	488	440	282	137	74	61	63	91	--	--	3,050
Hard maple	49	68	33	67	54	73	59	--	--	48	--	--	--	--	--	451
Soft maple	9	--	22	23	51	30	57	94	98	154	47	57	73	--	158	873
Ash	42	243	384	586	846	855	858	611	587	328	293	410	72	119	--	6,233
Cottonwood and aspen	1	5	20	57	91	170	220	343	326	369	226	170	409	508	3,297	6,210
Basswood	6	9	7	20	6	16	--	21	19	--	--	--	--	--	--	104
Black walnut	26	111	248	381	501	545	664	598	367	487	--	76	--	--	--	4,004
Other eastern soft hardwoods	377	1,180	1,613	2,093	2,075	1,937	1,817	2,143	1,505	930	931	429	602	654	1,358	19,645
Other eastern hard hardwoods	109	516	786	1,049	1,064	855	559	718	581	238	478	105	92	242	216	7,608
Eastern noncommercial hardwoods	250	675	1,191	1,113	1,247	797	466	300	373	462	230	171	171	144	225	7,814
All hardwoods	1,131	3,301	5,489	7,094	7,840	7,164	6,268	6,136	5,179	4,113	3,539	2,264	2,848	2,188	6,561	71,106
All species groups	1,209	3,494	5,802	7,498	8,141	7,445	6,432	6,287	5,179	4,113	3,539	2,264	2,848	2,188	6,561	73,001

All table cells without observations in the inventory sample are indicated by —. Table value of 0 indicates the aboveground tree biomass rounds to less than 1 thousand dry tons. Columns and rows may not add to their totals due to rounding.

Table 54.— Area of forest land, in thousand acres, by inventory unit, county, and forest-land status, Kansas, 2001-2005

Inventory unit and county	Unreserved forests			Reserved forests			All forest land
	Timberland	Unproductive	Total	Productive	Unproductive	Total	
Northeastern							
Atchison	25.3	--	25.3	--	--	--	25.3
Clay Center	69.3	--	69.3	--	--	--	69.3
Doniphan	38.9	--	38.9	--	--	--	38.9
Douglas	54.9	--	54.9	--	--	--	54.9
Franklin	49.0	--	49.0	--	--	--	49.0
Jackson	25.8	2.5	28.3	--	--	--	28.3
Jefferson	47.6	--	47.6	--	--	--	47.6
Johnson-Wyandotte	45.1	--	45.1	--	--	--	45.1
Leavenworth	92.7	1.3	94.0	--	--	--	94.0
Marshall	48.0	--	48.0	--	--	--	48.0
Miami	55.1	--	55.1	--	--	--	55.1
Nemaha-Brown	31.1	--	31.1	--	--	--	31.1
Osage	53.1	--	53.1	--	--	--	53.1
Pottawatomie	81.3	1.5	82.8	--	--	--	82.8
Riley-Geary	98.6	4.9	103.5	--	--	--	103.5
Shawnee	43.9	--	43.9	--	--	--	43.9
Wabaunsee	35.3	--	35.3	--	--	--	35.3
Total	895.2	10.2	905.4	--	--	--	905.4
Southeastern							
Anderson	21.2	1.3	22.5	--	--	--	22.5
Bourbon	67.5	--	67.5	--	--	--	67.5
Butler	39.2	--	39.2	--	--	--	39.2
Chautauqua	69.3	28.5	97.9	--	--	--	97.9
Cherokee	32.0	--	32.0	--	--	--	32.0
Coffey	50.8	--	50.8	--	--	--	50.8
Cowley	17.7	--	17.7	--	--	--	17.7
Crawford	58.1	--	58.1	--	--	--	58.1
Elk	10.6	--	10.6	--	--	--	10.6
Emporia	43.3	--	43.3	--	--	--	43.3
Greenwood	52.3	4.3	56.6	--	--	--	56.6
Labette	40.4	--	40.4	--	--	--	40.4
Linn	94.9	--	94.9	--	--	--	94.9
Montgomery	41.8	7.8	49.6	--	--	--	49.6
Neosho	34.2	--	34.2	--	--	--	34.2
Wilson	55.8	7.8	63.6	--	--	--	63.6
Woodson-Allen	49.7	--	49.7	--	--	--	49.7
Total	778.9	49.8	828.7	--	--	--	828.7

(Table 54 continued on next page)

(Table 54 continued)

Inventory unit and county	Unreserved forests			Reserved forests			All forest land
	Timberland	Unproductive	Total	Productive	Unproductive	Total	
Western							
Colby-Garden City-Dodge City	25.3	7.4	32.7	--	--	--	32.7
Great Bend-Hutchinson	76.5	--	76.5	--	--	--	76.5
Hays	68.2	--	68.2	1.5	--	1.5	69.7
Jewell-Mitchell	25.3	4.2	29.5	--	--	--	29.5
Republic-Cloud	55.8	--	55.8	--	--	--	55.8
Salina	37.5	--	37.5	--	--	--	37.5
Wichita	64.9	4.7	69.6	--	--	--	69.6
Total	353.6	16.3	369.9	1.5	--	1.5	371.4
All counties	2,027.7	76.3	2,104.0	1.5	--	1.5	2,105.5

All table cells without observations in the inventory sample are indicated by --. Table value of 0.0 indicates the acres round to less than 0.1 thousand acres. Columns and rows may not add to their totals due to rounding.

Clay Center = Clay, Dickinson, and Washington counties
Colby-Garden City-Dodge City = Cheyenne, Clark, Comanche, Decatur, Finney, Ford, Gove, Grant, Gray, Greeley, Hamilton, Haskell, Hodgeman, Kearny, Kiowa, Lane, Logan, Meade, Morton, Ness, Rawlins, Scott, Seward, Sheridan, Sherman, Stanton, Stevens, Thomas, Wallace, and Wichita counties
Emporia = Chase, Lyon, Marion, and Morris counties
Great Bend-Hutchinson = Barton, Edwards, Harvey, McPherson, Pawnee, Reno, Rice, Rush, and Stafford counties
Hays = Ellis, Graham, Norton, Osborne, Phillips, Rooks, Russell, Smith, and Trego counties
Salina = Ellsworth, Lincoln, Ottawa, and Saline counties
Wichita = Barber, Harper, Kingman, Pratt, Sedgwick, and Sumner counties

Table 55.—Area of forest land, in thousand acres, by inventory unit, county, ownership group, and forest-land status, Kansas, 2001-2005

Inventory unit and county	Forest Service		Other Federal		State and local government		Undifferentiated private		All forest land
	Timber-land	Other forest land	Timber-land	Other forest land	Timber-land	Other forest land	Timber-land	Other forest land	
Northeastern									
Atchison	--	--	--	--	--	--	25.3	--	25.3
Clay Center	--	--	--	--	--	--	69.3	--	69.3
Doniphan	--	--	--	--	--	--	38.9	--	38.9
Douglas	--	--	5.3	--	9.8	--	39.8	--	54.9
Franklin	--	--	--	--	--	--	49.0	--	49.0
Jackson	--	--	--	--	--	--	25.8	2.5	28.3
Jefferson	--	--	--	--	--	--	47.6	--	47.6
Johnson-Wyandotte	--	--	5.3	--	5.3	--	34.5	--	45.1
Leavenworth	--	--	6.4	--	--	--	86.3	1.3	94.0
Marshall	--	--	--	--	--	--	48.0	--	48.0
Miami	--	--	--	--	--	--	55.1	--	55.1
Nemaha-Brown	--	--	--	--	--	--	31.1	--	31.1
Osage	--	--	9.0	--	--	--	44.1	--	53.1
Pottawatomie	--	--	--	--	--	--	81.3	1.5	82.8
Riley-Geary	--	--	14.2	--	--	--	84.4	4.9	103.5
Shawnee	--	--	--	--	--	--	43.9	--	43.9
Wabaunsee	--	--	--	--	--	--	35.3	--	35.3
Total	--	--	40.3	--	15.1	--	839.7	10.2	905.4

(Table 55 continued on next page)

(Table 55 continued)

Inventory unit and county	Forest Service		Other Federal		State and local government		Undifferentiated private		All forest land
	Timber-land	Other forest land	Timber-land	Other forest land	Timber-land	Other forest land	Timber-land	Other forest land	
Southeastern									
Anderson	--	--	--	--	--	1.3	21.2	--	22.5
Bourbon	--	--	--	--	3.5	--	64.0	--	67.5
Butler	--	--	--	--	--	--	39.2	--	39.2
Chautauqua	--	--	--	--	--	--	69.3	28.5	97.9
Cherokee	--	--	--	--	5.2	--	26.8	--	32.0
Coffey	--	--	2.1	--	--	--	48.7	--	50.8
Cowley	--	--	--	--	--	--	17.7	--	17.7
Crawford	--	--	--	--	--	--	58.1	--	58.1
Elk	--	--	--	--	--	--	10.6	--	10.6
Emporia	--	--	2.6	--	--	--	40.6	--	43.3
Greenwood	--	--	12.1	--	--	--	40.2	4.3	56.6
Labette	--	--	5.2	--	--	--	35.2	--	40.4
Linn	--	--	--	--	7.8	--	87.1	--	94.9
Montgomery	--	--	--	--	--	--	41.8	7.8	49.6
Neosho	--	--	--	--	--	--	34.2	--	34.2
Wilson	--	--	--	--	--	--	55.8	7.8	63.6
Woodson-Allen	--	--	--	--	4.2	--	45.5	--	49.7
Total	--	--	22.1	--	20.8	1.3	736.0	48.5	828.7
Western									
Colby-Garden City-Dodge City	--	--	--	--	--	--	25.3	7.4	32.7
Great Bend-Hutchinson	--	--	--	--	--	--	76.5	--	76.5
Hays	--	--	--	--	--	1.5	68.2	--	69.7
Jewell-Mitchell	--	--	4.5	--	--	--	20.8	4.2	29.5
Republic-Cloud	--	--	--	--	--	--	55.8	--	55.8
Salina	--	--	6.0	--	--	--	31.6	--	37.5
Wichita	--	--	--	--	--	--	64.9	4.7	69.6
Total	--	--	10.4	--	--	1.5	343.2	16.3	371.4
All counties	--	--	72.8	--	35.9	2.8	1,918.9	75.0	2,105.5

All table cells without observations in the inventory sample are indicated by --. Table value of 0.0 indicates the acres round to less than 0.1 thousand acres. Columns and rows may not add to their totals due to rounding.

Clay Center = Clay, Dickinson, and Washington counties

Colby-Garden City-Dodge City = Cheyenne, Clark, Comanche, Decatur, Finney, Ford, Gove, Grant, Gray, Greeley, Hamilton, Haskell, Hodgeman, Kearny, Kiowa, Lane, Logan, Meade, Morton, Ness, Rawlins, Scott, Seward, Sheridan, Sherman, Stanton, Stevens, Thomas, Wallace, and Wichita counties

Emporia = Chase, Lyon, Marion, and Morris counties

Great Bend-Hutchinson = Barton, Edwards, Harvey, McPherson, Pawnee, Reno, Rice, Rush, and Stafford counties

Hays = Ellis, Graham, Norton, Osborne, Phillips, Rooks, Russell, Smith, and Trego counties

Salina = Ellsworth, Lincoln, Ottawa, and Saline counties

Wichita = Barber, Harper, Kingman, Pratt, Sedgwick, and Sumner counties

64

Table 56.—Area of forest land, in thousand acres, by county group, and forest type group, Kansas 2001-2005

							Forest type group					
County group	White-red-jack pine	Other eastern softwoods	Ponderosa pine	Oak-pine	Oak-hickory	Oak-gum-cypress	Elm-ash-cottonwood	Maple-beech-birch	Other hardwoods	Exotic hardwoods	Nonstocked	All groups
Anderson	--	3.4	--	--	9.4	--	9.7	--	--	--	--	22.5
Atchison	--	--	--	--	22.8	--	2.4	--	--	--	--	25.3
Bourbon	--	--	--	0.3	44.0	--	21.2	--	--	--	2.0	67.5
Butler	--	--	--	--	28.1	--	11.1	--	--	--	--	39.2
Chautauqua	--	--	--	--	97.9	--	--	--	--	--	--	97.9
Cherokee	--	--	--	--	15.3	--	16.7	--	--	--	--	32.0
Clay Center	--	1.5	--	--	26.5	--	28.9	--	2.0	--	10.4	69.3
Coffey	--	6.1	--	--	22.1	--	22.6	--	--	--	--	50.8
Colby-Garden City-Dodge City	--	--	--	4.5	12.2	--	14.4	--	--	1.6	--	32.7
Cowley	--	--	--	--	6.7	--	10.9	--	--	--	--	17.7
Crawford	--	--	--	--	39.4	--	16.1	--	2.6	--	--	58.1
Doniphan	--	--	--	--	37.7	--	1.2	--	--	--	--	38.9
Douglas	--	--	--	--	26.4	--	28.5	--	--	--	--	54.9
Elk	--	--	--	--	4.6	--	4.7	--	--	--	1.3	10.6
Emporia	--	5.2	--	--	28.7	--	9.4	--	--	--	--	43.3
Franklin	--	3.6	--	--	31.9	--	11.8	--	--	--	1.8	49.0
Great Bend-Hutchinson	--	6.5	--	--	31.7	--	27.4	--	8.4	--	2.5	76.5
Greenwood	--	--	--	--	22.4	--	29.7	--	4.5	--	--	56.6
Hays	--	2.2	--	--	27.5	--	35.0	--	--	5.1	--	69.7
Jackson	--	6.5	--	--	17.3	--	4.4	--	--	--	--	28.3
Jefferson	--	--	--	--	42.2	--	5.3	--	--	--	--	47.6
Jewell-Mitchell	--	--	--	--	14.9	--	10.2	--	4.5	--	--	29.5
Johnson-Wyandotte	--	--	--	5.3	39.1	--	0.6	--	--	--	--	45.1
Labette	--	--	--	--	25.3	1.3	13.8	--	--	--	--	40.4
Leavenworth	--	8.0	--	--	75.6	--	10.4	--	--	--	--	94.0
Linn	--	1.5	--	6.0	54.2	--	23.1	8.1	--	--	2.0	94.9
Marshall	--	--	--	5.2	20.4	--	22.3	--	--	--	--	48.0
Miami	--	--	--	--	25.3	--	22.2	7.6	--	--	--	55.1
Montgomery	--	--	--	1.1	42.4	--	6.1	--	--	--	--	49.6
Nemaha-Brown	--	0.7	--	--	19.7	--	10.6	--	--	--	--	31.1
Neosho	--	5.2	--	4.6	10.0	--	13.2	--	--	1.3	--	34.2
Osage	--	--	7.1	--	37.8	--	6.3	--	--	--	1.9	53.1
Pottawatomie	--	1.8	--	4.3	60.6	--	10.7	--	--	--	5.4	82.8
Republic-Cloud	--	--	--	4.7	27.1	--	24.1	--	--	--	--	55.8
Riley-Geary	3.1	13.9	--	9.2	55.9	--	21.4	--	--	--	--	103.5
Salina	--	--	--	--	20.3	--	8.7	--	--	6.4	2.1	37.5

(Table 56 continued on next page)

65

(Table 56 continued)

County group	Forest type group											
	White-red-jack pine	Other eastern softwoods	Ponderosa pine	Oak-pine	Oak-hickory	Oak-gum-cypress	Elm-ash-cottonwood	Maple-beech-birch	Other hardwoods	Exotic hardwoods	Nonstocked	All groups
Shawnee	--	--	--	--	40.7	--	3.2	--	--	--	--	43.9
Wabaunsee	--	--	--	--	21.4	--	13.9	--	--	--	--	35.3
Wichita	--	11.9	--	--	7.5	--	36.2	--	7.6	6.4	--	69.6
Wilson	--	--	--	--	48.6	5.2	9.8	--	--	--	--	63.6
Woodson-Allen	--	6.8	--	6.1	25.9	--	10.9	--	--	--	--	49.7
Grand Total	3.1	85.0	7.1	51.3	1,267.8	6.5	589.3	15.7	22.5	27.9	29.4	2,105.5

All table cells without observations in the inventory sample are indicated by --. Table value of 0.0 indicates the acres round to less than 0.1 thousand acres. Columns and rows may not add to their totals due to rounding.

Clay Center = Clay, Dickinson, and Washington counties

Colby-Garden City-Dodge City = Cheyenne, Clark, Comanche, Decatur, Finney, Ford, Gove, Grant, Gray, Greeley, Hamilton, Haskell, Hodgeman, Kearny, Kiowa, Lane, Logan, Meade, Morton, Ness, Rawlins, Scott, Seward, Sheridan, Sherman, Stanton, Stevens, Thomas, Wallace, and Wichita counties

Emporia = Chase, Lyon, Marion, and Morris counties

Great Bend-Hutchinson = Barton, Edwards, Harvey, McPherson, Pawnee, Reno, Rice, Rush, and Stafford counties

Hays = Ellis, Graham, Norton, Osborne, Phillips, Rooks, Russell, Smith, and Trego counties

Salina = Ellsworth, Lincoln, Ottawa, and Saline counties

Wichita = Barber, Harper, Kingman, Pratt, Sedgwick, and Sumner counties

Table 57. – Area of timberland, in thousand acres, by inventory unit, county, and stand-size class, Kansas, 2001-2005

Inventory unit and county	Stand-size class					All size classes
	Large diameter	Medium diameter	Small diameter	Chaparral	Nonstocked	
Northeastern						
Atchison	9.4	9.6	6.3	- -	- -	25.3
Clay Center	34.4	17.2	7.4	- -	10.4	69.3
Doniphan	16.5	22.4	- -	- -	- -	38.9
Douglas	35.1	15.9	3.9	- -	- -	54.9
Franklin	6.4	25.9	14.9	- -	1.8	49.0
Jackson	16.0	9.8	- -	- -	- -	25.8
Jefferson	19.3	25.1	3.1	- -	- -	47.6
Johnson-Wyandotte	28.0	11.8	5.3	- -	- -	45.1
Leavenworth	33.5	36.9	22.4	- -	- -	92.7
Marshall	26.6	12.8	8.6	- -	- -	48.0
Miami	41.6	8.1	5.3	- -	- -	55.1
Nemaha-Brown	11.1	15.9	4.1	- -	- -	31.1
Osage	21.1	23.2	7.0	- -	1.9	53.1
Pottawatomie	33.1	24.2	18.6	- -	5.4	81.3
Riley-Geary	33.2	24.1	41.3	- -	- -	98.6
Shawnee	21.0	22.9	- -	- -	- -	43.9
Wabaunsee	19.0	12.8	3.6	- -	- -	35.3
Total	405.3	318.5	151.9	- -	19.4	895.2
Southeastern						
Anderson	8.1	8.6	4.5	- -	- -	21.2
Bourbon	31.4	5.6	28.5	- -	2.0	67.5
Butler	12.3	21.6	5.2	- -	- -	39.2
Chautauqua	20.9	34.6	13.9	- -	- -	69.3
Cherokee	27.3	2.1	2.6	- -	- -	32.0
Coffey	24.0	14.7	12.1	- -	- -	50.8
Cowley	12.4	5.2	- -	- -	- -	17.7
Crawford	18.1	31.7	8.4	- -	- -	58.1
Elk	1.3	8.0	- -	- -	1.3	10.6
Emporia	26.2	13.2	3.9	- -	- -	43.3
Greenwood	33.3	15.1	3.9	- -	- -	52.3
Labette	20.4	14.0	6.1	- -	- -	40.4
Linn	29.1	61.8	2.0	- -	2.0	94.9
Montgomery	25.4	16.4	- -	- -	- -	41.8
Neosho	9.9	17.8	6.5	- -	- -	34.2
Wilson	7.9	35.4	12.5	- -	- -	55.8
Woodson-Allen	25.3	15.7	8.7	- -	- -	49.7
Total	333.4	321.2	118.9	- -	5.3	778.9

(Table 57 continued on next page)

(Table 57 continued)

Inventory unit and county	Large diameter	Medium diameter	Stand-size class Small diameter	Chaparral	Nonstocked	All size classes
Western						
Colby-Garden City-Dodge City	25.3	- -	- -	- -	- -	25.3
Great Bend-Hutchinson	43.9	28.7	1.4	- -	2.5	76.5
Hays	53.3	6.3	8.6	- -	- -	68.2
Jewell-Mitchell	20.8	- -	4.5	- - -	- -	25.3
Republic-Cloud	35.3	20.5	- -	- -	- -	55.8
Salina	7.7	27.7	- - -	- -	2.1	37.5
Wichita	39.4	7.3	18.3	- -	- -	64.9
Total	225.8	90.5	32.8	- - -	4.6	353.6
All counties	964.5	730.2	303.6	- -	29.4	2,027.7

All table cells without observations in the inventory sample are indicated by --. Table value of 0.0 indicates the acres round to less than 0.1 thousand acres. Columns and rows may not add to their totals due to rounding.

Clay Center = Clay, Dickinson, and Washington counties

Colby-Garden City-Dodge City = Cheyenne, Clark, Comanche, Decatur, Finney, Ford, Gove, Grant, Gray, Greeley, Hamilton, Haskell, Hodgeman, Kearny, Kiowa, Lane, Logan, Meade, Morton, Ness, Rawlins, Scott, Seward, Sheridan, Sherman, Stanton, Stevens, Thomas, Wallace, and Wichita counties

Emporia = Chase, Lyon, Marion, and Morris counties

Great Bend-Hutchinson = Barton, Edwards, Harvey, McPherson, Pawnee, Reno, Rice, Rush, and Stafford counties

Hays = Ellis, Graham, Norton, Osborne, Phillips, Rooks, Russell, Smith, and Trego counties

Salina = Ellsworth, Lincoln, Ottawa, and Saline counties

Wichita = Barber, Harper, Kingman, Pratt, Sedgwick, and Sumner counties

Table 58.—Area of timberland, in thousand acres, by inventory unit, county, and stocking class, Kansas, 2001-2005

Inventory unit and county	Stocking class of growing-stock trees					All classes
	Nonstocked	Poorly stocked	Moderately stocked	Fully stocked	Over-stocked	
Northeastern						
Atchison	15.9	4.4	4.9	--	--	25.3
Clay Center	24.5	21.5	13.5	9.9	--	69.3
Doniphan	1.2	24.8	8.6	4.4	--	38.9
Douglas	--	21.6	19.3	14.0	--	54.9
Franklin	6.1	16.7	23.7	2.5	--	49.0
Jackson	9.8	6.7	5.3	4.0	--	25.8
Jefferson	8.1	21.2	14.3	4.0	--	47.6
Johnson-Wyandotte	--	19.3	24.5	1.3	--	45.1
Leavenworth	2.7	43.7	40.0	3.2	3.2	92.7
Marshall	9.7	22.4	11.8	2.7	1.5	48.0
Miami	3.7	30.0	2.8	18.6	--	55.1
Nemaha-Brown	15.3	11.7	3.4	--	0.7	31.1
Osage	6.7	31.0	11.0	1.8	2.7	53.1
Pottawatomie	12.4	41.7	17.3	9.8	--	81.3
Riley-Geary	5.9	66.9	9.4	16.5	--	98.6
Shawnee	8.6	21.4	8.6	5.3	--	43.9
Wabaunsee	8.3	10.1	12.4	4.4	--	35.3
Total	138.8	415.2	230.6	102.5	8.1	895.2
Southeastern						
Anderson	2.1	4.7	10.1	4.3	--	21.2
Bourbon	13.2	42.6	1.3	9.0	1.5	67.5
Butler	12.1	19.4	7.8	--	--	39.2
Chautauqua	13.3	42.2	13.9	--	--	69.3
Cherokee	--	9.9	11.4	10.7	--	32.0
Coffey	12.1	14.7	3.9	20.2	--	50.8
Cowley	9.7	8.0	--	--	--	17.7
Crawford	20.5	18.6	6.0	13.0	--	58.1
Elk	9.3	--	1.3	--	--	10.6
Emporia	11.0	6.5	22.9	2.6	0.3	43.3
Greenwood	18.5	6.0	13.3	10.6	3.9	52.3
Labette	10.7	26.2	--	3.5	--	40.4
Linn	3.5	45.9	45.5	--	--	94.9
Montgomery	7.0	6.1	20.8	7.8	--	41.8
Neosho	5.9	11.9	--	16.1	0.4	34.2
Wilson	13.3	13.7	20.9	7.8	0.2	55.8
Woodson-Allen	4.0	21.0	24.6	--	--	49.7
Total	166.0	297.4	203.7	105.5	6.3	778.9

(Table 58 continued on next page)

69

(Table 58 continued)

Inventory unit and county	Stocking class of growing-stock trees					All classes
	Nonstocked	Poorly stocked	Moderately stocked	Fully stocked	Over-stocked	
Western						
Colby-Garden City-Dodge City	9.4	16.0	--	--	--	25.3
Great Bend-Hutchinson	21.4	27.4	21.8	5.9	--	76.5
Hays	31.3	20.6	7.8	8.5	--	68.2
Jewell-Mitchell	4.5	10.6	4.4	5.8	--	25.3
Republic-Cloud	16.1	23.8	11.2	2.9	1.8	55.8
Salina	14.8	15.0	7.7	--	--	37.5
Wichita	34.4	8.5	22.1	--	--	64.9
Total	131.9	121.9	75.0	23.1	1.8	353.6
All counties	436.7	834.4	509.4	231.1	16.1	2,027.7

All table cells without observations in the inventory sample are indicated by --. Table value of 0.0 indicates the acres round to less than 0.1 thousand acres. Columns and rows may not add to their totals due to rounding.
Clay Center = Clay, Dickinson, and Washington counties
Colby-Garden City-Dodge City = Cheyenne, Clark, Comanche, Decatur, Finney, Ford, Gove, Grant, Gray, Greeley, Hamilton, Haskell, Hodgeman, Kearny, Kiowa, Lane, Logan, Meade, Morton, Ness, Rawlins, Scott, Seward, Sheridan, Sherman, Stanton, Stevens, Thomas, Wallace, and Wichita counties
Emporia = Chase, Lyon, Marion, and Morris counties
Great Bend-Hutchinson = Barton, Edwards, Harvey, McPherson, Pawnee, Reno, Rice, Rush, and Stafford counties
Hays = Ellis, Graham, Norton, Osborne, Phillips, Rooks, Russell, Smith, and Trego counties
Salina = Ellsworth, Lincoln, Ottawa, and Saline counties
Wichita = Barber, Harper, Kingman, Pratt, Sedgwick, and Sumner counties

70

Table 59.—Net volume of growing-stock trees (at least 5 inches d.b.h.), in million cubic feet, and sawtimber trees (International 1/4-inch rule), in million board feet, on timberland by inventory unit, county, and major species group, Kansas, 2001-2005

Inventory unit and county	Growing-stock Major species group					Sawtimber Major species group				
	Pine	Other softwoods	Soft hardwoods	Hard hardwoods	All species	Pine	Other softwoods	Soft hardwoods	Hard hardwoods	All species
Northeastern										
Atchison	--	--	--	8.6	8.6	--	--	--	34.1	34.1
Clay Center	--	2.4	36.5	9.2	50.1	--	3.0	153.5	35.0	191.4
Doniphan	--	0.1	7.2	19.0	26.2	--	--	17.4	67.2	84.6
Douglas	--	0.8	43.7	18.4	62.9	--	1.1	184.5	63.4	249.0
Franklin	--	2.9	3.7	12.4	18.9	--	3.6	6.4	22.4	32.4
Jackson	--	3.7	3.9	8.6	16.3	--	14.8	11.2	33.8	59.8
Jefferson	--	0.2	16.6	15.2	32.0	--	--	53.2	49.9	103.0
Johnson-Wyandotte	--	0.7	1.6	30.6	32.8	--	1.1	--	121.1	122.2
Leavenworth	--	0.5	28.3	53.3	82.1	--	--	96.6	173.6	270.3
Marshall	--	1.2	18.1	13.2	32.5	--	1.5	83.0	52.8	137.3
Miami	--	0.8	30.0	34.7	65.5	--	3.9	134.2	124.5	262.6
Nemaha-Brown	--	0.1	3.1	3.7	7.0	--	--	6.1	7.3	13.4
Osage	2.1	0.8	8.2	10.5	21.6	4.3	--	29.8	16.2	50.3
Pottawatomie	--	2.1	5.4	21.2	28.7	--	3.5	12.3	80.6	96.4
Riley-Geary	4.0	4.5	21.2	22.9	52.6	14.3	10.6	62.3	91.8	179.2
Shawnee	--	1.0	20.4	15.6	36.9	--	1.7	61.6	58.9	142.2
Wabaunsee	--	--	33.1	13.1	46.2	--	--	146.5	42.5	189.0
Total	6.1	21.7	282.9	310.2	621.0	18.6	44.8	1,078.5	1,075.2	2,217.1

(Table 59 continued on next page)

(Table 59 continued)

Inventory unit and county	Growing-stock					Sawtimber				
	Major species group				All species	Major species group				All species
	Pine	Other softwoods	Soft hardwoods	Hard hardwoods		Pine	Other softwoods	Soft hardwoods	Hard hardwoods	
Southeastern										
Anderson	--	0.8	45.9	3.8	50.5	--	--	230.2	7.8	238.0
Bourbon	--	0.6	6.9	17.3	24.8	--	2.0	18.8	74.4	95.2
Butler	--	--	5.0	11.0	16.0	--	--	5.5	49.9	55.5
Chautauqua	--	0.3	1.0	18.9	20.2	--	--	--	52.8	52.8
Cherokee	--	--	20.0	26.5	46.5	--	--	86.0	109.2	195.2
Coffey	--	0.5	18.5	26.0	45.0	--	--	68.8	102.9	171.7
Cowley	--	0.8	1.1	3.4	5.3	--	3.0	2.1	14.9	20.1
Crawford	--	--	4.7	23.4	28.1	--	--	11.6	84.3	95.9
Elk	--	0.2	1.4	1.6	3.1	--	--	--	5.1	5.1
Emporia	--	1.7	35.1	13.9	50.6	--	2.5	154.5	58.9	215.9
Greenwood	--	0.2	31.6	13.1	44.9	--	--	114.6	37.6	152.2
Labette	--	1.3	14.1	7.8	23.2	--	1.9	53.1	18.6	73.6
Linn	--	4.7	11.8	51.2	67.7	--	15.2	34.4	153.5	203.0
Montgomery	--	--	12.7	25.8	38.5	--	--	43.5	89.8	133.4
Neosho	--	0.7	9.8	9.2	19.7	--	2.0	18.5	39.3	59.8
Wilson	--	0.4	16.1	21.8	38.3	--	--	66.6	71.4	138.0
Woodson-Allen	--	1.7	11.7	14.2	27.6	--	3.6	43.3	35.2	82.1
Total	--	13.9	247.5	288.8	550.1	--	30.2	951.7	1,005.6	1,987.5
Western										
Colby-Garden City-Dodge City	--	2.0	12.2	2.7	16.9	--	9.6	54.4	11.8	75.8
Great Bend-Hutchinson	1.9	5.7	78.0	16.4	101.9	8.4	23.4	339.9	57.0	428.6
Hays	--	0.1	36.6	9.8	46.4	--	--	160.0	30.6	190.6
Jewell-Mitchell	--	--	9.3	15.3	24.6	--	--	33.2	68.9	102.1
Republic-Cloud	--	1.8	16.4	24.5	42.7	--	8.1	64.8	101.2	174.1
Salina	--	0.1	8.5	11.2	19.9	--	--	26.8	42.4	69.2
Wichita	--	3.6	23.2	6.6	33.4	--	11.1	92.1	8.1	111.4
Total	1.9	13.3	184.2	86.4	285.8	8.4	52.2	771.3	320.0	1,151.9
All counties	8.0	49.0	714.6	685.4	1,456.9	27.0	127.2	2,801.4	2,400.8	5,356.5

All table cells without observations in the inventory sample are indicated by --. Table value of 0.0 indicates the volume rounds to less than 0.1 million cubic or board feet. Columns and rows may not add to their totals due to rounding.

Clay Center = Clay, Dickinson, and Washington counties
Colby-Garden City-Dodge City = Cheyenne, Clark, Comanche, Decatur, Finney, Ford, Gove, Grant, Gray, Greeley, Hamilton, Haskell, Hodgeman, Kearny, Kiowa, Lane, Logan, Meade, Morton, Ness, Rawlins, Scott, Seward, Sheridan, Sherman, Stanton, Stevens, Thomas, Wallace, and Wichita counties
Emporia = Chase, Lyon, Marion, and Morris counties
Great Bend-Hutchinson = Barton, Edwards, Harvey, McPherson, Pawnee, Reno, Rice, Rush, and Stafford counties
Hays = Ellis, Graham, Norton, Osborne, Phillips, Rooks, Russell, Smith, and Trego counties
Salina = Ellsworth, Lincoln, Ottawa, and Saline counties
Wichita = Barber, Harper, Kingman, Pratt, Sedgwick, and Sumner counties

Table 59a.—Net volume of growing-stock trees (at least 5 inches d.b.h.), in million cubic feet, and sawtimber trees (Doyle rule), in million board feet, on timberland by inventory unit, county, and major species group, Kansas, 2001-2005

Inventory unit and county	Growing-stock Major species group					Sawtimber Major species group				
	Pine	Other softwoods	Soft hardwoods	Hard hardwoods	All species	Pine	Other softwoods	Soft hardwoods	Hard hardwoods	All species
Northeast										
Atchison	--	--	--	8.6	8.6	--	--	--	19.9	19.9
Clay Center	--	2.4	38.5	9.2	50.1	--	1.0	105.0	28.7	134.7
Doniphan	--	0.1	7.2	19.0	26.2	--	--	11.7	44.6	56.4
Douglas	--	0.8	43.7	18.4	62.9	--	0.4	143.0	40.4	183.8
Franklin	--	2.9	3.7	12.4	18.9	--	1.5	2.7	10.1	14.3
Jackson	--	3.7	3.9	8.6	16.3	--	7.1	5.4	20.1	32.7
Jefferson	--	0.2	16.6	15.2	32.0	--	--	47.0	35.7	82.7
Johnson-Wyandotte	--	0.7	1.6	30.6	32.8	--	0.4	--	81.7	82.1
Leavenworth	--	0.5	28.3	53.3	82.1	--	--	101.6	115.3	217.0
Marshall	--	1.2	18.1	13.2	32.5	--	0.5	81.9	48.1	130.6
Miami	--	0.8	30.0	34.7	65.5	--	1.8	131.0	73.5	206.4
Nemaha-Brown	--	0.1	3.1	3.7	7.0	--	--	2.5	4.8	7.3
Osage	2.1	0.8	8.2	10.5	21.6	2.6	--	15.9	7.7	26.2
Pottawatomie	--	2.1	5.4	21.2	28.7	--	2.1	6.3	63.1	71.5
Riley-Geary	4.0	4.5	21.2	22.9	52.6	8.1	5.5	36.5	64.0	114.0
Shawnee	--	1.0	20.4	15.6	36.9	--	0.6	60.9	41.5	103.0
Wabaunsee	--	--	33.1	13.1	46.2	--	--	153.3	28.6	181.9
Total	6.1	21.7	282.9	310.2	621.0	10.6	21.0	905.0	727.8	1,664.4

(Table 59a continued on next page)

73

(Table 59a continued)

Inventory unit and county	Growing-stock Major species group					Sawtimber Major species group				
	Pine	Other softwoods	Soft hardwoods	Hard hardwoods	All species	Pine	Other softwoods	Soft hardwoods	Hard hardwoods	All species
Southeastern										
Anderson	--	0.8	45.9	3.8	50.5	--	--	225.1	3.9	228.9
Bourbon	--	0.6	6.9	17.3	24.8	--	0.7	10.0	58.2	68.9
Butler	--	--	5.0	11.0	16.0	--	--	2.3	44.7	47.0
Chautauqua	--	0.3	1.0	18.9	20.2	--	--	--	34.2	34.2
Cherokee	--	--	20.0	26.5	46.5	--	--	56.6	72.3	128.9
Coffey	--	0.5	18.5	26.0	45.0	--	--	52.4	72.7	125.1
Cowley	--	0.8	1.1	3.4	5.3	--	1.8	0.9	11.4	14.1
Crawford	--	--	4.7	23.4	28.1	--	--	5.7	74.4	80.1
Elk	--	0.2	1.4	1.6	3.1	--	--	--	2.4	2.4
Emporia	--	1.7	35.1	13.9	50.6	--	0.9	157.9	36.9	195.6
Greenwood	--	0.2	31.6	13.1	44.9	--	--	67.4	22.0	89.4
Labette	--	1.3	14.1	7.8	23.2	--	0.7	33.5	10.3	44.5
Linn	--	4.7	11.8	51.2	67.7	--	7.8	21.3	90.2	119.2
Montgomery	--	--	12.7	25.8	38.5	--	--	26.4	48.4	74.8
Neosho	--	0.7	9.8	9.2	19.7	--	1.0	8.3	24.8	34.0
Wilson	--	0.4	16.1	21.8	38.3	--	--	61.7	45.0	106.7
Woodson-Allen	--	1.7	11.7	14.2	27.6	--	1.5	24.7	18.4	44.5
Total	--	13.9	247.5	288.8	550.1	--	14.3	754.0	670.1	1,438.4
Western										
Colby-Garden City-Dodge City	--	2.0	12.2	2.7	16.9	--	5.7	38.5	6.4	50.6
Great Bend-Hutchinson	1.9	5.7	78.0	16.4	101.9	5.4	10.3	332.4	32.2	380.2
Hays	--	0.1	36.6	9.8	46.4	--	--	108.4	16.9	125.3
Jewell-Mitchell	--	--	9.3	15.3	24.6	--	--	18.8	49.4	68.2
Republic-Cloud	--	1.8	16.4	24.5	42.7	--	4.6	49.6	71.9	126.1
Salina	--	0.1	8.5	11.2	19.9	--	--	17.3	28.6	46.0
Wichita	--	3.6	23.2	6.6	33.4	--	4.4	67.6	4.6	76.5
Total	1.9	13.3	184.2	86.4	285.8	5.4	25.0	632.6	210.0	872.9
All counties	8.0	49.0	714.6	685.4	1,456.9	16.0	60.2	2,291.6	1,607.9	3,975.7

All table cells without observations in the inventory sample are indicated by --. Table value of 0.0 indicates the volume rounds to less than 0.1 million cubic or board feet. Columns and rows may not add to their totals due to rounding.

Clay Center = Clay, Dickinson, and Washington counties
Colby-Garden City-Dodge City = Cheyenne, Clark, Comanche, Decatur, Finney, Ford, Gove, Grant, Gray, Greeley, Hamilton, Haskell, Hodgeman, Kearny, Kiowa, Lane, Logan, Meade, Morton, Ness, Rawlins, Scott, Seward, Sheridan, Sherman, Stanton, Stevens, Thomas, Wallace, and Wichita counties
Emporia = Chase, Lyon, Marion, and Morris counties
Great Bend-Hutchinson = Barton, Edwards, Harvey, McPherson, Pawnee, Reno, Rice, Rush, and Stafford counties
Hays = Ellis, Graham, Norton, Osborne, Phillips, Rooks, Russell, Smith, and Trego counties
Salina = Ellsworth, Lincoln, Ottawa, and Saline counties
Wichita = Barber, Harper, Kingman, Pratt, Sedgwick, and Sumner counties

74

Table 65.—Sampling errors by Forest Survey Unit/County group for area of forestland, area of timberland, growing-stock volume on timberland, and sawtimber volume on timberland, Kansas, 2001-2005

Forest Survey Unit/County group	Area of forestland (acres)	Sampling error	Area of timberland (acres)	Sampling error	Growing-stock volume on timberland (cubic feet)	Sampling error	Sawtimber volume on timberland (board feet)	Sampling error
1 Atchison	25,262	44.29	25,262	44.29	8,603,177	69.75	34,124,825	68.15
1 Clay Center	69,350	24.94	69,350	24.94	50,083,003	46.26	191,443,345	52.85
1 Doniphan	38,931	33.84	38,931	33.84	26,223,493	38.91	84,617,082	43.66
1 Douglas	54,942	30.52	54,942	30.52	62,884,144	40.11	248,979,881	45.49
1 Franklin	49,035	31.25	49,035	31.25	18,931,918	42.63	32,354,570	56.35
1 Jackson	28,264	38.68	25,767	41.29	16,274,246	54.35	59,753,818	59.61
1 Jefferson	47,572	30.69	47,572	30.69	31,990,089	44.32	103,031,783	57.65
1 Johnson-Wyandotte	45,134	32.48	45,134	32.48	32,847,893	38.25	122,196,390	42.06
1 Leavenworth	94,044	22.47	92,707	22.44	82,130,664	36.63	270,286,904	45.39
1 Marshall	47,970	31.1	47,970	31.1	32,473,136	52.94	137,339,070	60.47
1 Miami	55,086	29.77	55,086	29.77	65,509,989	40.06	262,615,082	45.65
1 Nemaha-Brown	31,113	38.37	31,113	38.37	6,956,074	67.64	13,400,775	106.93
1 Osage	53,147	30.89	53,147	30.89	21,622,577	38.11	50,269,021	44.96
1 Pottawatomie	82,753	25.25	81,279	25.65	28,737,577	47.07	96,359,698	60.74
1 Riley-Geary	103,535	22.37	98,625	22.72	52,595,659	33.71	179,163,590	35.71
1 Shawnee	43,941	34.33	43,941	34.33	36,947,440	49.86	142,200,137	56.79
1 Wabaunsee	35,302	37.56	35,302	37.56	46,177,155	50.3	188,960,803	55.17
2 Anderson	22,544	38.38	21,238	40.21	50,549,360	80.78	238,001,382	86.65
2 Bourbon	67,487	27.79	67,487	27.79	24,835,438	45.42	95,248,915	52.88
2 Butler	39,200	35.7	39,200	35.7	15,963,786	49.48	55,461,697	61.46
2 Chautauqua	97,863	22.74	69,334	27.07	20,236,596	40.12	52,783,123	57.07
2 Cherokee	31,992	37.6	31,992	37.6	46,501,784	47.11	195,164,529	47.63
2 Coffey	50,848	31.13	50,848	31.13	44,997,777	47.49	171,690,676	52.07
2 Cowley	17,663	49.65	17,663	49.65	5,330,189	70.7	20,072,578	85.53
2 Crawford	58,131	28.4	58,131	28.4	28,080,061	48.4	95,907,429	56.73
2 Elk	10,567	56.95	10,567	56.95	3,092,941	73.46	5,067,524	108.1

(Table 65 continued on next page)

(Table 65 continued)

Forest Survey Unit/County group	Area of forestland (acres)	Sampling error	Area of timberland (acres)	Sampling error	Growing-stock volume on timberland (cubic feet)	Sampling error	Sawtimber volume on timberland (board feet)	Sampling error
2 Greenwood	56,640	32.02	52,299	32.64	44,882,665	45.96	152,229,442	49.62
2 Labette	40,420	34.51	40,420	34.51	23,191,448	47.65	73,605,240	61.92
2 Linn	94,947	23.45	94,947	23.45	67,660,370	27.99	203,049,526	33.81
2 Montgomery	49,619	32.38	41,790	34.93	38,496,461	45.4	133,368,124	49.18
2 Neosho	34,223	37.04	34,223	37.04	19,747,600	53.47	59,827,985	59.87
2 Wilson	63,593	29.21	55,764	31.47	38,327,186	46.58	137,997,443	56.45
2 Woodson-Allen	49,707	31.14	49,707	31.14	27,576,640	41.41	82,105,567	49.67
3 Colby-Garden City-Dodge City	32,734	37.71	25,336	42.59	16,924,115	63.89	75,795,130	67.33
3 Great Bend-Hutchinson	76,501	24.5	76,501	24.5	101,925,777	55.41	428,625,485	60.49
3 Hays	69,689	24.26	68,199	24.68	46,393,267	45.08	190,618,177	49.1
3 Jewell-Mitchell	29,514	39.25	25,284	42.66	24,560,618	53.69	102,092,897	57.25
3 Republic-Cloud	55,843	26.8	55,843	26.8	42,700,006	32.9	174,111,044	36.36
3 Salina	37,544	37.44	37,544	37.44	19,855,820	49.84	69,242,142	56.85
3 Wichita	69,590	26.94	64,937	28.03	33,440,817	41.24	111,396,995	46.9
All county groups	2,105,503	3.74	2,027,679	3.87	1,456,901,390	7.86	5,356,463,524	9.63

This report utilizes a sampling error based on one standard error which means the chances are two in three that had a 100-percent inventory been taken using these methods, the results would have been within the limits indicated.

Multiple county county groups:

Clay Center = Clay, Dickinson, and Washington counties

Colby-Garden City-Dodge City = Cheyenne, Clark, Comanche, Decatur, Finney, Ford, Gove, Grant, Gray, Greeley, Hamilton, Haskell, Hodgeman, Kearny, Kiowa, Lane, Logan, Meade, Morton, Ness, Rawlins, Scott, Seward, Sheridan, Sherman, Stanton, Stevens, Thomas, Wallace, and Wichita counties

Emporia = Chase, Lyon, Marion, and Morris counties

Great Bend-Hutchinson = Barton, Edwards, Harvey, McPherson, Pawnee, Reno, Rice, Rush, and Stafford counties

Hays = Ellis, Graham, Norton, Osborne, Phillips, Rooks, Russell, Smith, and Trego counties

Salina = Ellsworth, Lincoln, Ottawa, and Saline counties

Wichita = Barber, Harper, Kingman, Pratt, Sedgwick, and Sumner counties

76